Under the Tucson Moon

Also by Kim Antieau

Novels
The Blue Tail • *Broken Moon* • *Butch*
Church of the Old Mermaids • *Coyote Cowgirl* • *Deathmark*
The Desert Siren • *The Fish Wife: an Old Mermaids Novel*
The Gaia Websters • *Her Frozen Wild* • *Jewelweed Station*
The Jigsaw Woman • *Mercy, Unbound*
The Monster's Daughter • *Ruby's Imagine*
Swans in Winter • *The Rift* • *Whackadoodle Times*

Nonfiction
Counting on Wildflowers
The Old Mermaids Book of Days and Nights
The Old Mermaids Book of Days and Nights: A Year and a Day Journal
An Old Mermaid Journal
The Salmon Mysteries

Short Story Collections
Entangled Realities (with Mario Milosevic)
The First Book of Old Mermaids Tales
Tales Fabulous and Fairy
Trudging to Eden

Chapbook
Blossoms

Cartoons
Fun With Vic and Jane

Blog
www.kimantieau.com

Under the Tucson Moon

Kim Antieau

Green Snake
PUBLISHING

Under the Tucson Moon
by Kim Antieau

Copyright © 2013 by Kim Antieau

ISBN: 978-1-949644-28-9

All rights reserved.

No part of this book may be reproduced without written permission of the author.

Cover photos by Kim Antieau.
Bottom photo on back cover by Mario Milosevic.

http://www.kimantieau.com

Electronic editions of this book are available at your favorite ebook store.

Published by Green Snake Publishing
www.greensnakepublishing.com

In memory of my mom,
Mary K. Antieau,
and for all the desert creatures,
seen and unseen,
with love and special thanks to
Terri Windling,
Delia Sherman and Ellen Kushner,
and to all the EW caretakers.
I owe you so much.
Thank you.

CONTENTS

First 9

Year One: *Essays* 13
    Arrival 15
    There Will be Blood—& Coyotes 18
    Dog Days 21
    Coyote Dance 23
    In My Side 25
    Owls Want to Know 28
    Moon Over Tucson 30
    Getting it Right 34
    And Moi 38
    And the Weeping Woman 42
    Dreams of Love 53
    To Success 59
    Night at the Casita 64

Year Two: *Church of the Old Mermaids* 67
    In the Burning Ring of Fire 69
    Keep Going 72
    Fork in the Road 74
    The Old Sea 76

Year Three: *Old Mermaids Sanctuary* 81
    Rabies, Babies 83
    Songs of the Spirit 85
    The Pink Shoe 87
    Bridges 92
    Who? 99

Year Four: *The Blue Tail* 101
  Taking Care 103
  Night at the Old Mermaid Sanctuary 107

Year Five: *The Fish Wife* 115
  A Fool's Progress 117
  Barriers 119
  Regretting Endings 121
  Dreamy Desert Life 124
  Two Fairies at a Duster 127
  Fertile Old Moon 130

Year Six: *The Rift* 131
  Pilgrim 133
  By the Light 139
  Shimmer 144

Year Seven: *The Desert Siren* 149
  Sink or Swim 151
  The Wild Keeper 157

Year Eight: *Whackadoodle Times*
          Pricked: A Jane Deere Novel 167
  Walking in Prickly Beauty 169
  Thorny Palace 177

Year Nine: *The Monster's Daughter* 187
  The Monster's Daughter: An Essay 189
  Landed 197

FIRST

In the fall of 2004, I put out a call to friends and family, asking them to help me find a beautiful, environmentally safe place where my husband, Mario Milosevic, and I could stay for part of the winter. We live in the Pacific Northwest in an area where the winters are long, cold, rainy, and icy. I longed for sun and warmth.

As it happened, like a wonderful fairy goddessmother stepping in to save the day, Terri Windling answered my email and told me about a retreat in the Arizona desert she had helped create called Endicott West. I hesitated at first because we had lived in Tucson eighteen years earlier, and we had not enjoyed the experience. But Endicott West sounded peaceful and beautiful. Best of all, it had been designed to be a safe haven for writers, artists, and those who needed an environmentally safe place to shelter.

We started out driving to Tucson from the Columbia River Gorge where we live, but we had a car accident the first day out. Then we spent a week going from doctor to doctor and test to test to make certain Mario was all right because we weren't sure how the accident had occurred: Had Mario fallen asleep at the wheel or had he passed out? It was a harrowing week, and at the end of it, I got on a plane with Mario and we flew to Phoenix. I don't normally fly, and it wasn't a pleasant experience.

Eventually we made it to Tucson. The moment we opened the green metal door and stepped into the casita, I knew I had come home. Every nook and cranny, every wall, every door—all of it—was beautiful and meaningful. The place pulsed with mythos, magic, stories, and nature. It was as if it had been created just for me—for me and every creature, human or not, who sometimes needs a way station, a resting spot, a betwixt and between place to rest and recuperate before carrying on. Virginia Woolf wrote that every artist needs a place of her own. This was my place.

For the next nine winters, Mario and I came to Endicott West. We renamed it the Old Mermaids Sanctuary (after the Old Mermaids came out of the wash and gave me the stories for my novel *Church of the Old Mermaids)*, and we eventually shorthanded it to the Sanctuary. It was always wonderful *and* difficult to be at the Sanctuary. We looked forward to it every year.

During these nine years, my best friend died, two of our close friends died unexpectedly, I had two surgeries, I started and finished school again, I struggled with illness, depression, and identity, a family member struggled with drug addiction, a brother-in-law had a stroke, my father had major heart surgery, and my mother died. I also sold several books during this time, but then the bottom fell out of traditional publishing, and Mario and I became indie writers.

Also during this time our country was fighting two wars, our economy tanked, and we eventually elected a new president (and then re-elected him). Representative Gabrielle Giffords was shot in Tucson, and the country experienced numerous mass shootings, including Aurora and Newtown. Around the world, parts of Indonesia were crushed by the 2004 earthquake and tsunami, and

Japan endured an earthquake and tsunami that led to the Fukishima nuclear disaster, and oil poured into the Gulf of Mexico after the Deepwater Horizon disaster. The weather continued to go crazy. Wildfires burned up the West, Hurricane Katrina changed New Orleans and environs forever, Hurricane Sandy devastated the East, and monster tornadoes carved deadly swaths through the Midwest and Southern regions of the United States.

Sometimes it felt like the world was coming apart at the seams.

Through everything, I felt like I could survive and even thrive as long as I could eventually come to the Sanctuary with Mario.

I wrote hundreds of thousands of words during our writing retreats in Arizona and posted them on my blog. The first year I didn't write a novel, so I wrote more essays than I did the subsequent years. I had too many words to put in this volume, so I tried to include essays that showed who I was during each year and how I felt about being at the Sanctuary. Although I edited these essays a bit for sense, I tried to leave them as they were when I first posted them. I wanted the reader to see the evolution of my thinking, writing, and identity. Plus, each piece is of a particular time and place, and I wanted to honor that.

I went to the Sanctuary for healing. I went to find beauty and hope. Essentially I went to find myself again. I found the desert. I found myth in the desert, beauty in the desert. And I found stories. Oh, the stories I discovered—the stories the place told to me! I wrote down as many of them as I could.

Did I find healing, beauty, hope, and myself?

The desert changed me. That is how it should be. The land—place—always shapes me. It shapes all of us. I often say that I am a stenographer to the imaginal. Perhaps I am also a stenographer to the land. Perhaps I am a mouthpiece *for* the land. If that's true, I hope my words have done this place and my experience justice.

I'll leave that for the reader to decide.

Year One

Essays

ARRIVAL

December 30, 2004
We left Scottsdale on Thursday. Interstate 10 to Tucson is a four-lane highway, just as it was when we lived in Tucson 18 years ago. The first time we visited the Southwest, we drove this same stretch of highway in the dark in a drenching rain. We had never seen rain like that. The world became silver in an instant. We laughed nervously as we drove through the night and wondered if we would make it out.

On Thursday the traffic was practically bumper to bumper the entire way. One thing about traveling by car (or bus or train) is that you get to see the ugly parts of a city you really don't see when you fly. You see the industry that hangs onto the fringes of a town, usually polluting the poorer neighborhoods. You see wrecked cars heaped like metal turtles on a sunny log. You see junk and more junk and giant transmission towers making miles and miles of cat's cradle out of electric lines. It's a good thing seeing all of this. I don't believe in romanticizing a place—not until you get to know it. What kind of romance would it be anyway, if you only knew the good parts? It's easy to fall in love with a pretty face. If you love someone after you've seen her with snot on her face and knots in his hair, after you know what frightens him or makes her nasty, then that is true romance. Same with a place.

We drove until we came to the east edge of town, and that was where we found our writing retreat. Although I'm certain it must seem isolated to folks from the city, it is actually in a Tucson neighborhood. "Only they have dirt for lawns instead of grass," Mario said. We didn't care, as long as it was quiet, peaceful, and beautiful.

We went down a long dirt drive—cactuses crowding us every inch of the way—until we came to a one-story, flat-roofed desert house, adobe with blue trimming. On the north side, two horses stood on bare ground in two separate corrals. Desert surrounded the rest of the house. The young caretaker came out and showed us our casita, a small studio apartment attached to the house but with a separate entrance.

The casita is beautiful. In the large main room (which has a stone floor) is a queen-sized bed and two night stands. Across from it is a desk, with bookshelves next to it. Next to that, facing west, is a door that leads out to a walled porch/garden. Next to the door is a rocking chair, a kiva fireplace, a small wooden table with four chairs and another bookcase. Past the huge walk-in closet, we walk up to the kitchenette and the bathroom.

The entire place is an art piece. Every detail has been attended to. Vigas are overhead. The walls are creamy white. The doors are made from solid untreated wood, as are the window frames. The handmade tiles in the bathroom are green; the walls are purple.

Original paintings and drawings hang from the walls. Near the bed is a drawing of two people spooning. It's called "Sleeping Beauty" by Terri Windling. On one wall, in gold lettering, is a quote by Georgia O'Keeffe: "Art is a wicked thing. It is what we are." In the kitchenette, near the floor, is a tiny curved door. We opened it up and discovered a tiny (fake) mouse sitting inside.

The caretaker showed us the common area in the main house

and said the pool and hot tub were there for our use as well. Since the caretaker has a dog that kept barking at us, I guessed we wouldn't be using the common area much. I don't generally swim or use hot tubs, but I was intrigued by this pool. It was dark and inviting, as though holding a secret down below, rather than bright and chemicalized. I was surprised no painting adorned the bottom of it. From a palm tree in the pool area, two owls looked down at us. I thought that was a good sign.

We walked a short distance from the house, through the desert, to a tiny building called the Quail House. Inside was an easel, easy chair, book shelf with books, office chair, and a drawing table. Mario and I looked at each other and just grinned.

We had found our place.

THERE WILL BE BLOOD—& COYOTES

December 31, 2004
Woke up with a vicious headache. I mopped the floors with water (no soap). They weren't horribly dirty or anything. It's just something we usually do when we go somewhere: We clean a place so we can lay down our own dirt. Making the place our own. Nesting.

Later we found the nearest library branch (Bear Canyon) and got a library card and checked out books on local flora and fauna. We also got on the internet and printed off a copy of my editor's notes for *Mercy, Unbound.* I haven't decided if I'll work on it or not during our stay here. I kind of feel as though I've lost my mind, so I might work on fixing that instead. *Gotta find the tools for fixin' that, baby.*

We took a short walk along the wash. I was always told you should never walk in a wash (flash flooding), but we could see the hoof-, paw-, and footprints of many who had gone before us, and we figured they must know what they're doing. We heard quails *(wheet-wheet)* but did not see them. (At least I think they're quails. I remember the bobwhites in Michigan sounded similar, and they're part of the quail family.) We saw several rabbits, but they had small ears, so they weren't the lagomorphs of jackrabbit fame. A flicker or woodpecker flew by us, and a thrasher (shiny gray with yellow eyes and a curved bill) stood on the limb of a paloverde tree watching us.

Before dinner, Mario cut his finger. They didn't have any first aid stuff at the casita, so I jumped in the car and drove to Walgreens a few minutes away. (There's a Walgreens on every other corner here, it seems.) I got bandages, peroxide, and alcohol. I felt sick to my stomach. One thing after another keeps happening on this trip. If I were more relaxed, I might find it funny. I didn't. If one more thing happened, I felt like I'd snap. *Would I make a sound like a fresh string bean, or an old one? Or like a twig you step on during a hike? Or like someone snapping their fingers to a tune they like?*

The cut had not stopped bleeding by the time I got back. I wondered if Mario needed stitches. I'm in such overload from the car accident, Mario's tests, and the airplane ride that I don't have much perspective. Everything seems like a potential tragedy or disaster in the making. This being oversensitive is just crap; I am sick of it. Why can't we seem to change those things about ourselves that we despise? Perhaps it's a useless enterprise, after all, like trying to change the color of your eyes from brown to blue.

Mario's finger didn't stop bleeding for a long time. I finally relaxed enough to do a bit of pow wowing (a Pennsylvania Dutch healing method). A good pow wow can always stop bleeding, but I couldn't remember any of the chants. I had Mario close his eyes, breathe, and imagine the bleeding stop, the wound closing up, the red turning to pink. I changed one pow wow chant so that it had a desert bent. The crux of the story of the chant is that someone goes into the woods and finds three wells. By the time they get to the third well, the bleeding stops. I had Mario visualize walking through the desert. At the first well, by a saguaro, a desert fairy gives him permission to have a cup of water. At the second well, near a barrel cactus, another desert fairy gives permission for him to have half a drink. At the last well, which is dry, a desert fairy tells him the well is dry and his bleeding has stopped. (Only I had it rhyme somehow.)

Eventually the bleeding stopped and the wound closed up. Mario and I went out at dusk. The Sky was pink—for only a short time—as though the Earth had said something that embarrassed Sky, but only briefly; then it was back to falling for Night. We heard what at first sounded like fire engines. We stopped and faced the sound. It was coyotes howling. Bringing the sun down with their chorus of yips. Mario and I laughed. These coyotes howled with a distinct Southwestern accent—and they harmonized better than their cousins back in the Pacific Northwest.

DOG DAYS

January 1, 2005
Happy New Year! For breakfast, Mario made us potatoes, mushrooms, and eggs, all scrambled together. Afterward, we started to go outside via the pool area, but the caretaker's dog barked and came at me. I was so pissed. I had come here to rest and recuperate, to find my spirit again, maybe even my health, and a small semblance of sanity—and this damn dog barked every time I went any place on the property. This wasn't acceptable. And I told the caretaker so. I was so angry—I already said that, I know—because in the end I knew I would be blamed. *Oh, her. She's so much trouble. No one else cared about the dog. We don't want her back here. So much trouble. So unfriendly. She hates animals.* Blah, blah, blah! I'd heard it all before.

I knew the caretaker felt bad about what happened with the dog, and I felt bad about her feeling bad, but I didn't want to worry about this dog for three weeks. She said she'd put him in the barn. Of course then I had visions of this poor dog being cooped up because of me.

With my heart still racing from the fright the dog had given me, I went with Mario into the wash. We walked until we reached a dirt road. We were trying to find the entrance to the Saguaro National Park. We found dust and many dogs, one of whom decided to menace us. I swear if I'd had a gun, I would have pointed it at the first dog owner I came across. Let them feel what's it's like to be threatened. Which is one of the reasons I don't own a gun. . . .

We walked the long way home, to avoid the damn dog, then drove to the park. We saw a couple of jackrabbits. They're huge, about the size of a fox, with ears nearly as long as their bodies. They did not appear to be as timid as "regular" rabbits either, loping around like small kangaroos.

The hot water stopped working in the casita. *Trickster energy?* I stood in the middle of our room and called to the directions and asked if they could straighten out our vacation. We didn't want any jinxes, curses or whatever else was going on. First the car accident, then my computer crashed and cost major bucks to fix, Mario fell through a chair, a toilet got plugged, the "i" on my computer came off, Mario cut himself, we're living near a barking menacing dog, Mario got cactus needles in his hand, it's raining and flooding in a desert that's been in drought for five years, and the hot water went out.

It is kind of funny.

I suppose.

COYOTE DANCE

January 2, 2005
Cloudy and windy. Went to La Indita for breakfast. Stopped at a couple of bookstores. Nearly every time I go into a store here, I get a headache. Exhausted. Didn't sleep much last night. When we got home, I went and sat with my feet in the spa, a kind of hot tub connected to the peanut-shaped pool. It was quiet. White clouds covered the sky. I felt cottony. The wind rustled the dry leaves on the palm where the two owls sometimes come to roost. I heard no other sound except for that. I looked down at my feet in the water, flat against the indigo concrete steps in the spa. Felt myself begin to unwind. . . .

Mario came out and sat in a wooden swinging bench beneath a tree. I got up and sat in one of the weathered-gray lounge chairs. Clouds covered the sun, but it still gave off a bit of light and warmth. The wind moved the dry palm leaves (fronds?), and I closed my eyes.

I am so grateful to be here. Dog or no dog, hot water or no hot water, this is a beautiful inspiring place, and I am fortunate to be here.

I remained in that spot by the pool and in that position for an hour or more. I realized as I got up to go inside that it was the stillest I had been in years. The longest I had gone without doing *something* in years. *Even in my sleep I tossed and turned and kicked and growled, cried and created dreams no one would want.*

What was that saying? *I'm dancing as fast as I can.*

A coyote dance, I think.

Maybe I'll sit this one out. For a bit. I've got some re-creating to do.

IN MY SIDE

January 7, 2005

My dreams are peculiar here, more like movies than dreams. In one, a coach is telling a basketball player that he isn't giving one hundred percent. In another, Gene Hackman is trying to kill me with a knife. (Yes, I get it: hack man.) I awaken shaking and terrified.

I have strange rashes, along with the strange dreams. I itch almost constantly. One day at a park I took off nearly all of my clothes to find the source of the irritation. Didn't find it. Finally I lifted up my camisole and said to Mario, "What's going on?" Mario pulled a thorn from my side. I have no idea how a cactus thorn got under my clothes, since my clothes and I have not been rolling around in the desert. As far as I know.

But that's just a quibble. The news of the world fades away. The dog has settled down. Mario and I often go to sleep about 10:00 p.m., wake up ten hours or more later, then have breakfast. The sun shines. Or it rains. It is cold. Or it is warm. We walk the wash after breakfast. Gambel's Quail cluck, cluck, cluck as they run around in the underbrush before us. In the winter (like now), they form coveys (quail gangs, I say) and run together. Their bodies are plump, like other quails, and each has a plume on the top of its head. As they scurry about, they remind me of cloistered nuns trying to keep hidden, annoyed that I've trespassed on their sanctuary, yet unable to keep quiet or still about the entire thing. At night, the quails roost mostly in the paloverde, near bunches of desert mistletoe.

The desert mistletoe *(phoradendron californicum)* fascinates me. It's parasitic, so it gets at least part of its nutritional needs from its host, but it does have chlorophyll and photosynthesizes. It's green and segmented, looking like a spiky tinker toy project in clumps in the trees around here. I've seen them mostly in paloverde, but they're in other trees as well. They produce tiny red berries, which birds feed on (especially the phainopepla). The birds often fly away to another tree after dining on the mistletoe to wipe their beaks on a branch and get the sticky seeds off. The seeds also get eaten and become—intact—part of the bird droppings; thus the mistletoe finds a new host.

We see the silky-flycatcher *(phainopepla)* on our walks in the wash and around the grounds. It's smaller than a blue jay, but it has a similar shape, including the jaunty crest; only the phainopepla is indigo. Here in the Sonoran Desert, mistletoe berries are the main food source for the silky-flycatcher.

We also see other birds on our walks, along with a panoply of cactuses and other desert flora and fauna. We walk in desert sand, our feet making prints alongside the javelina prints from the night before, or the night before that. Javelinas are boar-like creatures who live in the desert and usually travel in packs, too. Their prints resemble tiny deer prints—or pig prints. We haven't seen them yet, only their tracks, several of them, running in a line from one part of the desert to another. Sometimes they stop and dig at something in the Earth, and then are off again. They eat prickly pear and often what they leave behind looks like a peculiar art piece: a mittened hand, heart, Mickey Mouse outline.

On our way back through the wash, we stop at the Quail House, the tiny studio I mentioned before. It's a small square building with a pointed roof. The green door can be closed all the way or the top half can be opened so that you can be in the studio and outside (kind of) at the same time.

To the east of us, we can see the Rincon Mountains, the tops of which are now dusted with snow. We often hike in the Saguaro National Park which slides up the Rincons. To the north are the Santa Catalina Mountains, also topped with snow. When we lived here, everyone just called them the Catalinas, and as long as you were in Tucson, you always knew where north was because of the mountains. At rush hour, the Catalinas would turn red from the pollution. I don't know if they still do that or not.

I am surrounded by beauty here. Sometimes it is so quiet I can hear myself breathe. Other times the annoying little dog next door won't shut up, I can hear the traffic on Speedway, and someone with a motor bike is missing the entire point of being out in Nature—and spoiling it for those of us who do get it. But it doesn't matter. I am getting into the flow of things. The dog didn't bark at me even once today.

And thus far, no more thorns in my side.

OWLS WANT TO KNOW

January 4, 2005
On Monday, clouds covered the sky at dusk, like massive bruises. I took candles out to the pool, and Mario and I sat on the edge of it with our feet in the warm spa. The lights from the city lit up the western sky. We went back into the casita just as it began to rain. Hard. We opened the door that leads to the porch and walled garden so we could listen to the rain battering the tin roof. We kept the door open while we slept, hoping to hear the coyotes. I awakened in the middle of the night to the sound of the coyotes howling. They sounded so close I thought they might be in our garden, conducting a serenade just for us. But I fell right back to sleep before I could get up and check or wake Mario up so he could hear.

I dreamed I was walking around naked, but I kept saying to people, "It's okay because I'm dreaming." I called someone on the phone for help and wasn't surprised to hear my own voice on the other end. I asked how to help myself and I answered, but I don't remember what I said. People kept looking at me, and I kept saying, "It's okay, it's only a dream. See, pinch me. It won't hurt." But when I pinched myself, I felt it. So I decided to get dressed. A clothes designer had to pick out what I should wear. It was late, though, and we had very little time before the fashion show. We went by a mannequin with a long black coat, a white short-sleeved top, and black pants. "Fabulous! Fabulous! That will be perfect," the designer said. I figured he knew what he was doing. I suggested a strand of pearls to go with it, and he agreed. This was all rather amusing, seeing I'm not much of fashionista. In the morning, I awakened to the sounds of the owls in the palm tree, inquiring, "Who? Who?" *Who are you? Who, who, who, who?*

MOON OVER TUCSON

January 7, 2005

Strange day.

Killer bees attacked a group of joggers in the park near us where we've been hiking nearly every day. Freakin' killer bees. Two of the joggers had over 600 stings between them. 600 stings! I'd like to know who was counting.

They call them "Africanized" bees now instead of killer bees. Pray tell why? They *are* killer bees. Three people died in Arizona last year after they were attacked. But my question is why are they Africanized? As far as I can remember some whack job scientist who should have known better in South America was experimenting with bees and *oops* some of them got loose. (Have these scientists never watched a Saturday afternoon B science fiction movie? THEY ALWAYS GET LOOSE!)

Mario and I were on our way out of town today to visit the old Tumacacori mission when I heard about these bees. I never worried about killer bees before, but now they're half a mile from where I'm staying! (Truth is, I have worried about them before. When I first heard about them years ago I worried. But then, I'm a worrier.)

We stopped at a visitor center to get a forest service pass, and they told us that "problem" mountain lions were running around

Sabino Canyon, the other place we've been hiking. Are they really dangerous, I wondered? Apparently they've been exhibiting "aberrant" behaviors, such as stalking humans and talking on cell phones in movie theaters. Do you know what to do if you see a mountain lion? Don't run. *Hah!* Really. *Don't run.* It triggers their chase instinct. Don't crouch or bend over. Never look away. What are you supposed to do if attacked? Try discussing the federal deficit with it. It'll confuse the shit out of the lion.

And what to do to avoid being attacked by killer bees? Every single article I've read says you should avoid killer bees to avoid getting attacked. *Oh really?* Particularly their hives. But not a single article describes what those hives look like. This all sounds like it comes from the "duh" file.

I found all this rather funny as we drove out of Tucson and passed some lovely little strip mines, stuck behind a vehicle that was spewing white toxins in the air as I was first having an asthma attack and then an allergy attack.

I don't like missions, particularly, or churches, since I think missionary work is basically abhorrent, but the Catholic Church often built its churches on sites that were considered sacred by those they were trying to convert. When I visited Tumacacori years earlier, I remembered hardly anyone else being around. I walked through the church and looked up at the blue sky and down at patches of grass and flowers at my feet. It had been a cool oasis away from the hot desert. It wasn't like that today. Lots of people were around. The church had a roof. No flowers. Just dirt and dreariness. Maybe we had gone to a different church?

Mario and I decided to drive a little further south to just before the Mexican border, to a lake in the Coronado National Forest where we hoped to do some bird-watching. We drove into the forest for a few miles, but nothing sparked our interest: The hills were dry and nearly bare. When we reached the lake, we learned it was a fake lake (dammed), so we decided to return to Tucson.

On the way back to the freeway, a roadrunner ran across the road in front of us. (What were they called before there were roads?) We stopped the car to watch it. This was only about the third roadrunner I had seen in real life. They're big birds, with streaked brown feathers and a long tail that angles up so that the bird is shaped like a laid back "u." It has a long beak and tufted hair on top of its head.

Roadrunners can fly but they usually run—up to 15 mph. They eat snakes (as well as insects and other things), and they can jump into the air to catch low-flying birds or insects. The one we saw today moseyed away from us, looking here and looking there before it blended in completely with the landscape. Some First Peoples consider roadrunners sacred because you can't tell whether they are coming or going from their tracks.

In a scat and track book under scat for roadrunners, the author wrote, "None ever found." Mario wondered if we would be hailed by the scientific community if we found roadrunner scat. I said, "Be all that you can be."

We were back home before dusk. Mario took a nap, and I walked the wash. On the way back, I heard an owl hoot. I also heard a very peculiar noise, as though some creature were in distress. I noticed the vet was in with the horses, but when I asked the caretaker about the noise, she said she had gone outside when she heard the sound and stood under the tree. She said the sound definitely came from the owl. Just as she told me this, the owl flew away to begin its nightly hunt.

After dark, Mario and I went to campus to hear a lecture by Lynn Margulis on the Gaia theory. Her talk was part of a series of lectures called "Astrobiology and the Sacred." They had a large auditorium booked for such a distinguished scientist, but apparently the campus police had locked the hall, and we couldn't get in, so they moved the lecture to a classroom in the observatory. En masse a hundred or so of us walked up from the underground building to the observatory, a stream of people going with the flow.

Margulis began her lecture with a quote from Emily Dickinson. She had Mario and I hooked from then on. I didn't understand everything she talked about, but she says that evolution by increments (i.e. mutations) can't be the only way life acquires new adaptations. She showed how some organisms take other organisms into their bodies and don't destroy the other but instead incorporate some of their characteristics. It's called symbiogenesis. She says that "new tissues, organs and even new species evolve primarily through the long-lasting intimacy of strangers." For instance, one species of slugs ingests an organism that is capable of photosynthesis; after that, the slug takes all its nutrition by photosynthesis. Fascinating stuff. What if we could do that? Wouldn't that be revolutionary?

On the way back to the retreat, Mario and I remarked on how invigorating it is to learn new things. Isn't it? The world seems different afterward. I thought about how I had wanted to study biology at one time. I still sometimes think about going back to school and studying a science. Maybe even go to Amherst, where Margulis and Emily both come from.

Mario and I drove down Speedway with the radio turned up. I rolled down the window and looked up at the stars as we went by chain store after chain store after chain store.

"Look, honey," I said. "It's new moon. You can see the stars."

GETTING IT RIGHT

January 11, 2005

Mario and I lived in Tucson from September 1985 to September 1986. We drove into town towing a U-Haul trailer filled with our meager worldly goods (mostly books) and our cat Lockheart. We had barely a dime between us.

We found a motel with a kitchen, parked the U-Haul, then drove around town trying to find a place to live. One of the first things we saw was a man running from an apartment building holding a very large gun. No one seemed alarmed except us. This did not seem like a good sign. We learned the Air Force had illegally dumped toxic chemicals, so several city wells were contaminated. A man was breaking into homes around 8:00 p.m. to rob and rape. The press dubbed him the Prime-Time Rapist. The sun was so hot it burned the skin I was thinking of growing in the future.

Every place we could afford to rent was a dump. Squalid, seedy, scary. When I went to get my scholarship money, they told me I only got half of the money now and the rest halfway through the semester. Oh, and the bank took a cut. We had been counting on ALL of the money to get a place to live (first, last, and a security deposit). We worried we might soon be homeless.

I was a couple of days out of a small town on the coast of

Oregon, and I felt slapped silly with culture shock. I don't think I ever got over that bad beginning.

We finally rented a tiny apartment in a giant apartment complex at the edge of town. We had no furniture—and we never got any. We slept on the floor for a long while until we saved enough money to buy a futon . . . which we put on the floor. It raised us a few inches off the carpet. We had a tiny black and white television set a friend had given me when I was in college. We put Mario's mother's old kitchen table in the living room, but it had no chairs. I had my typing table (which I still use) and an old office chair. Mario set up a card table in the walk-in closet for his study, but we don't remember what he used as a chair. We had ceiling to ceiling and nearly wall to wall bookshelves (filled with books) in the living room. We sat on the carpet to watch TV.

I didn't like the apartment complex, but at least the apartment was clean. I never met another person, not even the people who lived around us. The lawn was grass, and it seemed like the sprinklers were on all the time, but they missed most of the lawn and watered the concrete sidewalk instead.

Around rush hour, a reddish haze would begin to settle around the nearby Catalinas. Mario rode his bike to work, and I imagined him breathing in those car fumes every day as he went to and from work. I was often stuck in traffic as I left school for home. Our car didn't have any air conditioning so being in stop-and-go traffic was what I imagined hell was like.

I started work at my part-time job as a teaching fellow soon after we arrived in Tucson, but the salary was so meager it barely paid for groceries. I was in school full-time, so Mario had to get a full-time job. He went out every weekday morning for a month, eight hours a day, looking for a job. Every morning he got the newspaper, circled the classifieds, then went looking. He did this every day from morning to night ,day after day after day.

Arizona is a "right to work" state which appears to mean that employers can pay you squat and make you do whatever they want and you are supposed to smile and say thank you. Most places wanted Mario to take a lie detector test and/or a drug test. Mario told them they could test his job performance all they wanted, but he wasn't taking a lie detector test, and they weren't getting any of his blood or urine. (Mario has barely told a lie in his life, and he doesn't drink or do drugs, but that was hardly the point.) Some days after he came home without finding a job, I thought, just take the damn drug test. But I never said it out loud. I agreed with him. After a month, he got a job as a typesetter.

Now that we're in Tucson again, Mario and I look back at our year in Tucson and wonder what we did during that time. My entire focus was on going to school and getting through in a year so that we could leave again. We didn't like the heat or the pollution, so I think we spent a lot of time in our apartment. We didn't notice any of the natural beauty surrounding us because of the red haze, I suppose. Or maybe because we didn't have any money to pay for anything, we never went anywhere. When we lived here, we never knew about Saguaro National Park or the Rincon Mountains or Sabino Canyon. I knew about the Catalinas because we lived in the foothills of the foothills of them.

We were fish out of water here then. We never got our bearings. We never even went to the Grand Canyon while we lived in Arizona. We never drove over to New Mexico. I can remember only a couple of things we enjoyed doing while we lived here. On hot nights we liked driving up into one of the neighborhoods north of us, just a couple minutes away. We'd park our car, sit on the hood, and watch the heat lightning above the city. The lights of the city shimmered as if it were all a mirage. (Yes, just like the scene in *Coyote Cowgirl*.) We liked the sunsets, too. We would walk to the "trail" (i.e. sidewalk) along the wash behind the apartment complex and watch the pink light slide along clouds that stretched across the sky like a bunch of gaudy feather boas thrown into the air.

But I started getting sick after we had been in Tucson only a few months. All of my energy went into trying to finish school and get out of town before I got any sicker. I blamed getting sick on Tucson. I was sure once we hit the road again, I would leave whatever ailed me behind in the desert.

I didn't. But that's another story.

Now I'm back here and looking at it all anew. I appreciate the area now more than I did then, although it still has some serious problems. (The word sprawl comes to mind. And strip mining. Come on, who does that shit? There are forty-two Walgreens here, along with five Walmarts, eighteen Safeways, eleven Starbucks, and eighty-eight Circle K's.)

I don't know if Tucson made me sick all those years ago. I wish I had found some comfort when I lived here then. But that's water in the wash, so to speak. Here and now I'm glad for the coyote chorus each night, owls in the palm tree, skies at sunset I can't even begin to describe, quail coveys, empty washes, and saguaro yoga.

Thomas Wolfe said you can't go home again. I never thought of Tucson as home all those years ago, so I can't say, technically, that I've tried to come home. I have tried to come back to some sense of myself. I have felt at home here, at times. (Mario is here, and his presence always makes home a possibility for me.) Yet home has to be wherever each of us is, doesn't it? If we can be at home in our bodies, we will be at home wherever we go.

I'm not quite home in my body yet, but I'm working on it. I'm thinking tomorrow morning I'll go out in the desert and do a little yoga with the saguaro. That should get my mind and body right.

AND MOI

January 12, 2005

It's cold tonight. Mario and I saw the crescent moon, like the smile on a Cheshire cat, just before it slipped below the horizon. The horses are wearing blankets to keep warm. This fascinates Mario. He wonders if they really keep the horses toasty, and I tell him, "Sure, as long as they don't wander too far from the outlets and accidentally unplug the blankets." He looks at me quizzically for a moment. I can't keep a straight face. Sometimes it's just fun to tease the former city boy.

I have bonded with one of the horses. When I arrived here, three perfectly healthy horses lived in the corrals several yards away. Now one is sick. We'll call her Colette. I used to know horse breeds when I was a horse crazy girl, but I don't any more. Colette is probably a quarter horse, or some mix of a quarter horse and something else. She's a dark chestnut color with a bit of white on her forehead and several small patches of white across her withers.

I noticed a couple of days ago that she was a little lethargic. The horse she shares corral space with, a gelding, was being bossier than usual. Whenever we went over to give them carrots, the bully never let Colette eat. Ears flat against his head, teeth bared, he'd go after her if she tried to get her share. So Mario and I decided not to go over with treats any more.

The vet came over the day Colette was looking lethargic and did some nasty things to her, sticking hoses here and there and everywhere. Apparently the owners had been out riding and Colette tried to jump a small creek instead of walking across it and she got caught in quicksand. (When Mario heard this, he said, "Quicksand? So you're telling me there's killer bees, problem lions, AND quicksand!") Colette hit her underside when she went into the quicksand, so they were worried she may have messed up her stomach. Horses can have problems with their tummies. For one thing, they can't throw up.

First thing I did this morning was look out the window to see how she was doing. A minute later, she went down. I waited. She wasn't on her side. Her legs were under her, her head up, her ears forward. After I got dressed, I went out and told the owner I'd be home most of the day so I'd keep on eye on her. She thanked me, and we talked about how many times Colette had pooped last night. (Three times.) She hadn't eaten for 36 hours straight, but she was eating now.

The caretaker's dog came running up behind me while I was talking. I turned around, and he crouched down: ready to spring up and play. I put my hand out and said, "I don't want any dog boogers." I couldn't help but laugh at how ridiculous this dog looked preparing to play or pounce on me, whichever activity I gave him permission to do. He ran away again when he realized I was having none of it. At least he isn't barking at me any more.

After the owner left and Mario went to the Quail House, I went outside to the fence. Colette's head went up as soon as she saw me, and she came over to the fence. As long as the bully saw I didn't have any treats, he stayed away. Colette lifted her head over the fence and let me put my hand on her forehead. I tried to do Reiki on her. I've done Reiki on animals before (dogs, actually), and they seemed to respond to it by becoming almost completely still. Colette did the same thing. She didn't seem to care whether I had a treat or not. She appeared to want the company. She stayed with me for a while and then the bully came over, so I left before there was an altercation. Colette didn't need that.

I came out off and on all day, in-between reading and making corrections on my book coming out from Aqueduct Press, *Counting on Wildflowers: an Entanglement.* Colette kept putting her head and neck through the fence, reaching toward the little bits of grass outside the corral. It seemed she wanted some fresh food. I smuggled her some carrots and a few bits of clover I could find. I didn't want to give her any other "greens" since I don't know my desert plants well enough to cause her no harm. She nearly always came to the fence when I came out, something she had not done before she was sick. I went over and tried to give her a little healing and a little loving each time. Sometimes when I watched her through the window of the casita, she looked so lethargic I was afraid she was worsening, but then the other two horses looked lethargic, too. How much fun could it be to spend all day in this corral with no grass to eat, no pleasant company, not even a book to read . . . or eat?

When I was a girl, I had an imaginary world where the girls (and women) had enormous political, social, and magical power. I had my own planet in this world, where I lived with many, many horses, and my best friend, Palo. Everywhere we went, we went with our horses. Our home planet was called 2,000, which was code for Horse. I was absolutely undeniably horse crazy when I was a girl. I slept with the book *Black Beauty* under my pillow in the hopes I would dream of horses. I read *The Black Stallion* books by Walter Farley over and over, although I wished Alec had been a girl instead of a boy.

Despite all of this, I was afraid of horses. This was not something I ever told anyone. My aunt had been thrown from her horse as a girl, and she was permanently paralyzed on one side of her face. Plus, horses were big animals; I was a little girl. That did not dim my passion, however. I went to places where I could be with horses as often as I could.

Puberty came, however, and my horse fetish went out the window. And as I've gotten older, I've grown more and more uncomfortable with domesticated animals (and the implications of animal slavery therein). Although I have sometimes wanted to start riding again, I haven't been able to convince myself the horses like being ridden, so I haven't done it.

I find it rather amusing that I come to the desert for some wild healing, and I stumble upon a sick horse, and for some reason, we like each other. It ain't world peace or nothing. But it was a shared peace, between two creatures, for a few hours today. I hope Colette is better in the morning

And I hope she kicks the bully's butt.

AND THE WEEPING WOMAN

January 16, 2005

Sometimes I am completely still here. I sit by the pool and listen to the wind blowing through the palm tree. I watch the sleeping owl as the tree sways ever so slightly. Sometimes a sound will cause her to open her eyes and rotate her head so far around I start thinking *Exorcist*.

Sometimes we all need a little exorcism. . . . Or is that exercise?

Did I tell you owls have feathers that make no noise when they fly so that prey cannot hear them coming? At least that's why the biologists say their wings make no noise. How do they know they didn't evolve silencer feathers so they wouldn't be distracted by their own noises while they flew above the world?

I imagine a princess who has lost her memory wandering into the house and out to the pool. She sits by the pool and looks up at the owl in the palm tree. And then the owl is standing across the pool from her, only she is an owl woman, made of soft comforting feathers the color of the shadows on the moon. The princess says she has forgotten who she is or how to help herself or anyone else. The owl woman asks her to look into her eyes and tell her what she sees, "I see myself. Only different." "Go out into the desert every day for three days," the owl woman says.

"When you are finished come tell me what you find." For three days, the forgotten princess goes out once a day and walks in the desert. She sees many things: cacti, roadrunners, coyotes, horses, quail, cardinals, feathers, fumets, prints in the sand. But she can't really say she has found any of those things. They all existed before she did. Near the end of the third day, she breathes deeply and looks down at her hands. Her hands! She recognizes her hands. She hurries back to the pool where the owl woman awaits her. *"What is it you found?"* the owl woman asks. *"Myself, myself, myself!"* she cries. *"I remember who I am. I found myself."* The owl woman nods, then flies up toward the palm tree . . . or becomes a shadow on the moon, awaiting the next one who is forgotten.

I am so still sometimes that the cactus wrens come and walk by my feet. They are spotted and streaked in brown, as if Nature didn't quite know how she wanted them to look. Sometimes I see flickering red, and I know the cardinal is in one of the trees on the other side of the wall. Other times I hear music coming from the tall tree next to the house—tall for here, that is. I think it's an old mesquite tree. The music is a bird song, many different bird songs, actually; sometimes the bird even repeats the words "ribbit, ribbit," over and over, as if it has dreams of being a frog. When I look through the binoculars, I think it is a mockingbird whose throat moves up and down with song. Maybe a thrasher. Gila woodpeckers sit on top of saguaros, looking all around, as if contemplating their domain. "Top of the world, Ma!"

Mario goes to the Quail House and plots. Literally. A couple of weeks into the process he tells me some of the story. I grin and say, "Oh, I wish I'd thought of that." It is the ultimate compliment one writer can give another. As for me, I'm storied out, I think. I want more: I want to know that my stories will make a difference in my life. I want healing from them.

My friend Linda gets her teeth pulled, most of them, in preparation for weekly chemo. Some of them were bad, the teeth, so the docs didn't want an infection to stop the chemo. My other friend with the brain tumor has been diagnosed with another brain tumor. Mutt and Jeff he calls them. Different agencies argue over which one will foot the bill for the life-saving chemo while he writes poetry and waits to see if they'll let him live. Colette, the horse, gets better. I wonder how I can be happy here when so many suffer. How can I have healing when so many are ill? Linda says, "That's your Judeo-Christian guilt stuff coming up. You deserve happiness just as much as anyone else does." When I asked a Buddhist therapist once to tell me why I deserved to be healthy when my mother was still ill, she said that question was an example of my hubris. I didn't understand. I still don't.

I walk the wash, sometimes with Mario, sometimes alone. We see all kinds of footprints. Some we recognize. Some canine prints are huge. We wonder if they grow coyotes bigger out here. One big print looked like bear, but we don't believe bear are here. Some looked feline in nature. *Jaguar, can you whisper to me the secrets of the ages?*

We walk in the wash at dusk, when La Llorona, the Weeping Woman, is said to wander along riversides or in washes, looking for her lost children. I listen for her moans but only hear my own breathing.

Sometimes we drive far out into the Sonoran desert. One day we go to the Buenos Aires National Wildlife Refuge. We follow a curved road through desolate cumin-colored hills. Mesquite covers many of the hills, an indication that this country either still is or has been range land. Cows eat the mesquite pods, then poop out the seeds (seeds which love being in the alimentary system of the cows); then the mesquite propagates more than the proverbial reproducing rabbits. Then ranchers use pesticides to kill the mesquite (rather ineffectively). Arguments rage on all sides (or at least on some sides) about whether mesquite is a pest or a boon. I can see the dilemma. When they aren't taking over the landscape and creating their own monoculture, the mesquite trees are beautiful, spirited, reaching deep deep down into the desert earth to find water.

We find a marshland—a real life wetland—in southern Arizona at the refuge. Tall dry marsh grass makes the wetland blond at this time of year. The bare cottonwoods are tall and ghostly, their branches curving up as they reach for the sky, frozen, as though caught in mid-dance. A small blackish bird, maybe a Black Phoebe, sits on a reed in a marshy pond, coming down from her perch every few minutes to scoop something out of the water.

Two cardinals, the male resplendent in his red Zoot suit of feathers, dart from bare branch to bare branch in the forest just behind the marsh. A hawk or harrier flies overhead. A flock of birds rises up from the marsh; we see their pale yellow underbellies just before they drop back down again, hidden by the grass, reeds, and cattails. Maybe Western Kingbirds? On the trail, we find bones of a deer or pronghorn, its small hooves curled up toward the leg bone as though it were still in the womb, still waiting for life. I hear red-winged blackbirds but do not see them.

Later, we leave and drive past Arivaca and many Border Patrol SUVs. This is jaguar country—or at least we hope it is. This is the absolute northern part of the jaguar's range. Sometimes they cross the border and come up into Arizona, although biologists don't believe there are any breeding pairs in the United States. I would love to see this giant spotted cat (even the black ones are actually black spotted). They are power, mystery, and ability incarnate. Often in Meso-American myths, they represent death or darkness. In my mythos, they are just beautiful.

Mario and I stop at another trail. As we prepare to step out of the car, an Anglo man walks toward us, a gun on his hip, and says, "Have you seen a bunch of illegal aliens come this way?" Mario and I look at each other, wondering silently, "How would we know?"

"No," I say, "we haven't seen anyone."

"I just rustled me up about six back there," he says, as though he's talking about cattle or birds or something not quite human.

"Are you with Border Patrol?" I ask, since he has a gun.

"No," he says. "It just makes me mad. You know that car that overturned the other day in Arivaca that sent those illegals to the hospital, we paid for that."

Mario and I get out of our car. I frown, but I don't say anything. My momma didn't raise me stupid: I ain't gonna aggravate this white man with a gun. But I'm thinking, I'd rather pay for medical care for so-called illegal aliens than for dropping bombs on Iraq.

"If you see a couple of ladies, one's my wife," he says as he gets into his huge white truck with Montana license plates. "Tell her I'll be right back."

"Why are you carrying a gun?" I ask.

"I never go out into the desert without protection," he says. He drives off.

He carries a gun, but he's running off to find the Border Patrol and leaving his wife behind?

"Are you worried?" I ask Mario.

"About what?" he asks. "A bunch of guys trying to find jobs?"

I nod. "I agree. But this guy with the gun could hurt someone."

We go for our walk amongst old cottonwoods along a dry streambed. Several of the huge old trees have fallen across the bed, as though they just got too tired to stand it any more. We wonder how the guy with the gun knew the men were illegals. He had seen brown people out in the woods, that was it? Since he was from Montana maybe he didn't understand that brown people had been here longer than any Anglos. . . .

We see several shoe prints in a wash off of the trail and wonder if these are the prints of the "aliens." I hope they have enough water.

We drive again. In the distance, mountain ranges rise on the right and left of us. Is that West and East? I've lost my bearings. We can see the observatories of Kitt Peak, tiny domes on a flat "peak." Why do we call this landscape desolate? Magnificent desolation. Didn't one of the astronauts say that about the moon? Kitt Peak is on reservation land. Before they put the 'scopes up there, the scientists had to convince the tribal elders that what they were doing wouldn't desecrate the mountain. They brought several of the elders to Tucson and had them look through the telescopes here. The elders said, (and I'm paraphrasing), "You are the people with the long eyes." They liked what they saw and decided the observatories would not be a desecration. So the scientists were able to build their telescopes a little closer to the stars.

Another day, we drive to a small town in southwest Arizona to see a gathering of sandhill cranes. Instead we find an ugly little desert town, like something out of an apocalyptic Australian film. It's technogarbage in the desert. Car dealerships. A fertilizer factory. A tank of pesticides on every other block. I try not to be judgmental, try to understand why people live in places without art or beauty—or live with art and beauty I do not see. We drive past mile after mile of barren farm fields and pesticide containers. We finally see art in the form of a mural on the side of a barn depicting a plane flying over a field spraying pesticides.

We cannot drive away fast enough. The road takes us to the Chiricahua Mountains. The brochure at the visitor center says it is the "place in the United States where the Rocky Mountains meet the Sierra Madre and the Sonoran Desert meets the Chihuahua Desert." It is part of the "sky islands" of Arizona, mountains popping up in the middle of deserts or grassland seas. At Massia Point, we get out and walk the trail. Red and cream-colored rocks surround us. We walk toward the edge and are astonished to see—all around the tree-filled valley below—columns of balanced rocks seeming to look forward, like tall rock giants gathered together at tribal council. Stone elders. The Apache called them "standing up rocks." Mario and I sit and listen, watch. I whisper my thanks and prayers to them.

We leave the Stone Elders and drive toward another refuge, although it appears we are traveling in the direction of where a power plant sits, belching out smoke that rises in the air like an ancient smoke signal, "Come here, come here."

We turn right at the power plant. Across the road from the power plant is an area that they (the power plant mucky mucks) have set aside for bird watching. Sandhill cranes winter at a body of water about a quarter of a mile or more away. We stand on the cement viewing area, in this place between Nature and technology, and look at thousands of sandhill cranes. We hear them first, the sound like the reassuring murmur of the Earth. We luxuriate in the sound, in knowing thousands of these birds live. In the fall, hundreds of the cranes are hunted and killed here, for sport. No one eats cranes. But some people kill them for the fun of it.

We dance the crane dance as we leave, arms moving slowly and elegantly up and down.

Away from the cranes and cardinals and whispers of jaguars, we sit in a Guatemalan restaurant in Tucson. A huge mural on the wall depicts a scene from Guatemala: the deep blue mist of the place, the waterfalls, women walking. I imagine jaguars live in those misty blue spaces on the wall. The family who owns the restaurant fled Guatemala after the father was imprisoned and tortured. What is it like to be so far from home? To be on the edges of this or that culture? I talk with the woman who waits on us. She has been here since she was 11. Although she has returned to Guatemala for a visit, her parents are still too frightened to go home. Recently the president who was responsible for so much of the torture and slaughter ran again for office, but he was not elected. I am grateful for the woman's easy conversation, for her allowing me to hear the history of her life.

I eat potatoes and mushrooms from the inside of a chile. Mario sips lemonade and eats spinach and walnut patties. I look at the colorful cloth on the walls around us and feel at home. I want to cry.

We go to Antigone, the bookstore down the street from the restaurant. I look at all the beautiful books and wonder what stories are within. One book is about how the body remembers, even if our conscious mind doesn't. I used to believe that. Now I'm not so certain. Now I wonder if everything is just as we see it, just as we know it, with nothing underneath. No mystery. Imagination is just imagination, not the healing flow of the Divine within each of us. Stories are just stories. Nothing more. Other times I agree with Muriel Rukeyser: "The world is made of stories, not atoms." This night, I sink into a chair in the bookstore and start to cry—although I don't know why. I wipe my eyes quickly, prepared to tell anyone who might ask that it's just allergies.

We go to campus after dinner to look at the first photos taken by a lander on Titan. Many of the scientists who worked on the project were from the University of Arizona. The hall is packed with people so we can't see anything. The scientist talking sounds very excited. We see a member of our peace group there with his family. Visiting Tucson just like us. Talk about a small solar system. We say hello, are amazed for a bit; then he has to run and check on his kids. Mario and I go outside where several telescopes have been set up on the mall. Saturn is especially close now. I look through one of the powerful 'scopes and see

Saturn and its rings. I am so excited. I have never seen them that clearly before. "Look, look," I want to yell. "Isn't this marvelous? Isn't life grand?"

On the way home, I turn up Pat Benatar singing, "Heartbreaker," and I sing it loud, dancing as best I can inside the car. Mario laughs, happy in my happiness, and I kiss him as he drives down Speedway. What a gift it is to be loved.

Today, Sunday, we walk the wash at dusk. We take the dog with us. He licks my hand (the dog, that is), and I don't even try to wash it away—even though I know where that tongue has been. (Let's not think about it.) No owl hoots tonight. Even the quails are silent. On the way back, near the house, a quail rustles in the tree and then flies away, startling us. I guess they can't figure out that if they just stayed still, we'd never figure out they were there! Mario and I kiss, then part company. He and the dog go toward the house. I head for the mesquite tree near the Quail House.

I sit under the mesquite tree and tell a story, out loud. It is a ritual I do every day, near dusk, near the threshold time, when some believe the veil is lifted between then and now, here and there. A borderland. Usually I don't know what I'll say until I sit down. Tonight I sit in one of the rusty chairs under the tree and start the tale:

> Once upon a time stories were told about a woman who walked the wash that runs through the desert near the old mesquite tree. She nearly always wandered through the wash at dusk, crying and moaning. They called her La Llorona, the Weeping Woman. Parents warned their children to stay away from the wash because La Llorona might mistake them for her lost children. She killed her children in anger after her lover and their father left her for another woman. A

younger richer woman. Or maybe she didn't kill her children. Maybe they just died and she was looking for more children. Some people said that her crying and weeping didn't have anything to do with children. In fact, she didn't have children. She was crying because there was no water in the wash, and there was no water because there were too many people in Arizona and they were desecrating the land.

Well, one night, the Mesquite Spirit heard what sounded like moaning and crying coming from the wash. The Spirit had been here a long time and hadn't ever seen La Llorona, although the stories had been out there just as long. But the Spirit went into the wash and was surprised to see a weeping woman standing in the sand. "La Llorona," the Spirit said. "Why are you crying?" She wiped her eyes. "I don't know," she said. "I've been wandering this wash for so long that I've forgotten why I cry." "Could it be because you killed your children to punish your lover?" She looked at the Spirit. "That sounds pretty stupid, and I don't think I'm stupid, so no, I didn't kill my children." "Hmmm. Are you crying because your children are dead?" "That would be a good reason to cry," she said, "but I don't think I ever had any children." "Ahhh, so you cry because there is no more water left in the desert." She thought about this and finally shook her head. "No, I don't think that's it either." The Spirit said, "I will take you to the end of the wash and out onto the road and then maybe you will remember."

Together they walked down the wash past the paloverde by the house. Several quails shook the bushes, cried out, then flew in front of the woman and the Spirit, startling them both. They continued walking by several mesquite trees. More quails cried, flapped their wings, and flew in the faces of the startled beings. Weeping Woman started to cry again. "What is it?" the Spirit asked. "Why are you crying?" "I remember now," she said. "I was trying to get to the other side of the wash and those damn quails kept flying out and scaring me half to death. I got so confused I couldn't remember which way was home." The Spirit took her out of the wash and set her on the path to home. And that was the last anyone heard of La Llorona, at least in that particular wash.

When I finish the story, I am laughing. I stand and thank the Mesquite for listening. I am still in the borderland of story time. Yes, that's it. Stories are part of the borderlands. Edge dwellers. Like jaguars and weeping women wandering the wash. Stories are incantations whispered, said aloud, sung. Are they incantations that ultimately heal us? Stories help us step over the threshold into . . . our lives. Or sometimes they help us step out of our lives. Help us get perspective like the Gila woodpecker looking over his domain. I have told stories since before I could write. *Don't I have this ability for a reason?* It doesn't have to be a cosmic reason. It can be practical. It can be medicine. Will I ever know? *Let the mystery be.*

I hurry through the dusk-colored desert toward the house. The dog jumps out, startling me, eager to play. I say, "Good dog," and then I go into the casita where Mario awaits.

DREAMS OF LOVE

January 23, 2005
I keep falling asleep as I'm writing about my older sister and me when we were kids and about an uncle who babysat us but did not care for us. It is nearly dark, and I give in to the sleep and fall on my side thinking of my older sister and how I love her, how we allow each other to remember our own lives without censorship. We shared that time with my uncle, but I cannot remember it because I was too young. I've always encouraged her to talk about it, despite all the other fingers to the lips that warned, "Shhhhh!"

Outside the owl is *hoo-hooing,* as it had been all day yesterday, then quiet today, now dusk and it is calling out, and I can tell it is calling out for something—someone—and I fall to my side, eyes closed, and my sister and I are reaching for this bird as it falls out of the tree, reaching to save it, only it is on the ground with us, right side up, blinking, and it is an owl, white with spots. A spotted owl. *Endangered.*

I open my eyes from this fugue dream and sit up and see the gray that dusk is tonight even though last night was a spectacle, with clouds in so many shapes and colors I was certain an artist was behind it all, but tonight I see the gray and hear the owl. I step outside and hear a low moan, then another owl, two owls now and the palm leaves are moving up and down, reminiscent of that old saying "don't come knocking if this trailer is a rockin'" and I'm certain some owl lovin' is going on even though I haven't a clue as to how owls actually mate. I wish Mario, who is back home in Washington, was with me to eavesdrop on these wild things doing the wild thing.

The nearly full moon rises above the Rincons. I go out toward the wash, and I think about a playwright I heard on NPR yesterday. I can't remember her name. But she said we each had a right to our own story. No matter who doesn't like it. No matter who tries to make us tell it differently. It is ours. She also said that every childhood is traumatic. All the more reason to tell the tale?

Is that true, I wonder, that every childhood is traumatic? I was frightened so much of the time, but no one ever knew. I know this because I've asked. At night I hid from my parents so I wouldn't have to sleep and face the demons in my dreams. During the day, I sometimes hid until the bus and my father drove away so I wouldn't have to go to school and face the teacher who promised to whip us if we didn't behave. Yet I stood nose to belly button with bullies. I wrestled with boys who gave me lip. When I look back at my childhood, it was one long quest for safety and happiness—the search for the grail. And I was the hero, always. Each child is, isn't she? My sister tried to protect me from a child molester. I tried to protect my younger sister from bullies. My younger sister tried to live through daily taunts and bullying and frustration because she could not learn the way others learned.

I think of all this as I go out into the wash. The moon is the eye on an alligator cloud. The wash feels dangerous tonight. All the canine prints look like giant wolf prints, hungry for Little Red Riding Hood, only I'm Little Blue Riding Hood. (What does that mean? Red hood when I was a girl, blue hood now that I'm older?) The man prints are prints of psychopaths, surely. Nevertheless I will not let any of them take the wash from me. It is my sea on the shore of the desert. The pale dirt has the consistency of sand. Cactus guts ride the dry middle like flotsam thrown up on the beach. Too much dog shit, just like at the beach. I am La Llorona, gnashing my teeth and wailing as I stride through the wash. It grows darker by the second. I remember rattlesnakes come out at night, and I just learned today they don't always rattle before they strike which is something I have believed since I was a child listening for that rattle as I ran through the woods near our house, hearing it at least once and telling my sisters to run, run home, while I stayed behind to peek at the snake, her head raised, tail up, the rattle swinging back and forth so fast I could barely see it, me feeling the thrill of being that close. . . .

Now the coyotes howl in the distance.

I left Mario at the Sky Harbor Airport in Phoenix on Friday. I cried so hard I could barely see. People turned to look at me. I couldn't find my rented car in the ocean of other white cars so I used the panic button on the key chain. The car beeped and flashed its lights. Everyone in the garage was looking around in a panic. Except me. I was relieved.

As I drove away, I saw the smog that had settled over the city, nothing like Carl Sandburg's fog coming in on little cat's feet, unless this was a mutant cat spewing out smoggy breath. I got to my parents' (currently unoccupied) townhouse in Scottsdale but couldn't get the key to work. I went from door to door, lock to lock. I was about to leave when I tried it one more time, scraping my hand as the door finally opened. Now I was bleeding and I went to the sink to wash my hand but there wasn't any water.

When my brother-in-law came home from a long hard day, he made me organic scrambled eggs along with potatoes, peas, chives, onions, garlic, tarragon, all cooked in olive oil. It was a great kindness and I appreciated it. I saved half of it for breakfast the next morning. I couldn't sleep, so I got up at 11:30 p.m., packed up my breakfast, and drove to Tucson. I put gas in the car myself, for the first time in many years (because of the fumes). On one stretch of road with four lanes, I was nearly the only one on it. It felt great. Adventurous. (Thelma and . . . Thelma. No, wait, I'm more Louise. That was Susan Sarandon, right?)

I got to Tucson about 1:30 a.m. The police were out in force, blocking off several streets. It had rained in Tucson, so the streets were wet, and the street lights seemed strange—preternatural in a way I can't explain except everything looked *fine*, as though I were in a *One Step Beyond* episode, but it would be all right. I hit nearly every green light on Speedway for about twelve miles. The moon was out, reflected in the pools of water on the side of the road. Cotton ball clouds shared the sky with Tinker Bell stars. I was dreaming by 2:30 a.m., falling asleep almost immediately, not thinking about Mario not being with me. The next day, everything was difficult. Everything I did hurt. I felt half here, as I always feel when I'm away from Mario, as though I'm a ghost, just going through the motions.

Which brings me to the wash tonight, me determined to walk through the monstrous hordes of wolves, coyotes, javelinas, alligator, rattlers, memories. I make it back to the casita, whole, unscathed. I know I was there because the quails flew away at my approach and the rabbits hopped away, each tail like a white version of the red light at the end of a train.

The first week or so we were at the casita, the caretaker had a dream about me. She said the wolves and coyotes were howling and I went outside in the dark—she could hear my feet crunching over the desert sand—and the wolves and coyotes stopped barking and howling and she wondered how I did that and also thought what I was doing was a bit dangerous. My own dreams in the beginning were vivid and odd. Some were nightmarish. Dreams have always been a part of my life in a way I've never understood. I had my first nightmare when I was about four and then the nearly nightly occurrence of nightmares was a staple for me for decades. I've never understood them and have come to believe they must be a way I relieve stress or blow off steam, or something. Sometimes they are metaphoric and I understand their messages; often I don't.

What do owls dream about? Do they understand love, life, death? As I walked through the wash tonight, I also thought of death. I heard late last night that another person I knew died suddenly, maybe even from asthma; they're not sure yet. A few days earlier I had cried in Mario's arms, telling him that death was horrible and it wasn't easy or beautiful and I didn't know how to live with this knowledge. Do animals think about death or understand it? Instinctively they try not to get hurt or to become prey. Is that the same thing as consciously thinking about one's own death?

Today I was thinking that loving someone is such a brave and wonderful thing to do. Being part of a community is a brave and wonderful thing to do, too. Loss is an inevitable part of life. If we remain separate, life is probably far less painful. Yet it is probably not as joyful. I don't like feeling like a ghost when I'm away from Mario, but I'm not going to stop loving him so that I don't feel that way. Someone asked me how come I know so many dying or sick people. I said, "Because I know people." It is inevitable. That doesn't mean it isn't difficult. It's part of going with the flow of life—which I certainly haven't mastered. I heard a poet on NPR (Paul Levine?) who is 70 and he said he thought by his age he would have acquired some wisdom, but he didn't feel as though he had. I laughed because I feel the same damn way.

Tonight the wash was full of danger: gray and spooky. Last night it was full of magic, mystery: red and mystical. Probably the only thing different in the wash was me. One night I saw the talons of mortality swooping down on me and everyone I love. Another night the talons were nothing more than the artist's brush painting the night sky.

Maybe it's all a dream.

Tonight, Mario and I are going to try and dream together. Meet at Falling Creek in our dreams. It is almost Full Moon. A time to dream. Time for owl love.

Or any other kind of love.

Sweet dreams.

TO SUCCESS

What is healing but a shift in perspective?
—*Mark Doty,* Heaven's Coast

Give sorrow words.
—*William Shakespeare*

January 27, 2005
Wednesday

Some bad days. Crappy nights. I had three or four good days and then yesterday I got sick: trouble breathing, bad headache, bad bad allergy attack, anxiety (shouldn't wonder). I was so scared I packed up and was ready to head out for Phoenix, where I would at least be near my sister. But I went outside and the clouds had cleared enough for the full moon to come out. The yard was silvery, you know that way strong moonlight makes a place look, like daylight but not quite, dreamier. I drove out to the end of the drive and a coyote ambled by, not concerned with me at all. I thought, well, maybe it'll be okay. I drove down the road a couple of miles to a trailhead at Saguaro East. My breathing loosened up a bit. So I went back to the casita.

It was not an easy night, however. Or an easy morning. In and out of sleep and misery. To be sick is one thing. To be alone and sick is another. I bow down to all of you who do it regularly. I'm in awe.

The night before, I was in bliss. The sky was clear, the stars out, the moon full of reflection, the coyotes howling. I danced around the casita to—what else?—"Coyote Dance." The caretaker came and got me to look at a herd of javelinas in the front yard through the bedroom window. At first I thought I was looking at cactuses, but then the little cactuses scurried away and the big long pig-like cactus moved and I saw his snout. I was so excited. Then I went outside and stood in the light, unable to dance or talk or do anything but be in that spot, buttressed by the beauty of it all.

Then all hell broke loose the next morning. Haven't a clue why.

Finally got out of bed midday and drove to town to get something to eat. It had been raining off and on all night and day. I filled the tank with gas, then went to this vegetarian restaurant reviewers semi-raved about. It's been around forever and its menu is at least part vegetarian. I got out of the car feeling dizzy and fragile. Called Mario. "How am I going to get back home?" I asked. "How am I going to stay here for another week? How will I get to Phoenix?" He tried to reassure me; then I went into the restaurant.

The table was sticky, the floor was filthy, the menu dirty. I ordered anyway, since I was feeling so shaky. I went outside to get the paper and they locked me out. I couldn't believe it. They were supposed to be open until 10 p.m. Finally after I banged on the door a few times (only because I'd left my book inside), a man opened the door and said, "Ma'am, we closed at 2:00 p.m. today." I said, "I've got an order in." He reluctantly let me back in. I sat at the table looking around and felt more and more uncomfortable. So I got up and left.

It occurred to me as I was banging on the restaurant door to get in that during this trip issues with keys have come up again and again. Keys and locks and doors. The rental car does not have a place to unlock it with a key on the passenger side. In fact you can't unlock it except from the driver's side, which is strange and not at all convenient. None of the locks in my parents' townhouse worked easily, and I ended up hurting my hand trying to get in. The locks on the casita don't work well either, and I'm constantly having trouble getting in or out. The license plate on the car is: KYS.

What is the key to all of this? What is the key to my healing? Or what is the key to acceptance?

I decided to go to the Guatemalan restaurant and thought I knew what I was doing but I ended up driving around for half an hour, quite lost. Somehow I managed to find the restaurant. I read the paper and ate, then went to Antigone, the great feminist bookstore down the street from the restaurant, to get a book I'd ordered, but it wasn't in yet. I shopped at the co-op across the street. A homeless man asked if he could help with the groceries. I said, "That's really sweet, but I need to work on my upper body strength." It occurred to me after that he needed money. I could have used his help, actually, since I was lugging water. I really do need to work on my strength. I know this sounds like a grocery list of "things Kim did today," and it is, but it's extraordinary, too, because I don't do a lot of these ordinary kinds of things at home, especially not after being so sick. I was pleased I could do them all.

It was sprinkling when I got back to the casita. I saw the caretaker and dog, but I was shaky and shy, often a reaction I get after being sick. Normal interactions are difficult. You know how you feel when you've been in the dark and then you come into the light and the light hurts? It's like that.

I decided to take a walk out into the desert despite the rain. It was nearly sunset, but I went up a trail in Saguaro East. It was so quiet, still. The sand was red mud in places. Drops of water hung from some of the cholla, completely still, as if they were part of the cactus. I heard and saw several Gila woodpeckers, noisy little creatures on top of the saguaros. On the ground was a prickly pear pad, partially shriveled, shaped now like a shell; in the "shell" part was a tiny pool of water with sand in it, just like a shell at the beach, a reminder once again that this had all once been an ocean.

My how the times they are a-changin'

Thursday

Better night but still not up to par. Feel all wrung out. Allergies really bad and scary. Someone better suited should have been given this job. . . .

Spent much of last night trying to figure out how to get home. The train tracks north of LA have been washed away? Well, actually the land *underneath* the tracks has washed away, as a good humored agent explained to me. I talked to many different Amtrak agents. Most were not good humored; they were automatons. I hate that. You can be a human being. I've worked in public service all my adult life. If people can't be human, they should get a job where they don't have to be human. Whatever that is. I thought about flying home or driving. But I guess I'll stay with the train, even though that means I'll be in a bus for half the day. Bleck.

When I spent the summer backpacking through Europe when I was eighteen, public transit was so easy. Their trains were great; their buses were great. None of them had that chemical smell/taste that our public transit often does. They were roomy, comfortable, on time. And they went everywhere. Amtrak doesn't go to Phoenix, Arizona, one of the biggest cities in the United States. Of course, it doesn't go to San Francisco, either. Or Santa

Fe. You have to get off the train and onto a bus to get to any of those places.

I know I'm whining.

Really, I'm just feeling sorrowful. Sorrowful at my own failures as a human being. I think because I don't know what triggers these episodes—was I exposed to pesticides, did I eat something I shouldn't have, did I come in contact with some chemical, is it the phase of the moon, did I think something I shouldn't have, did I not jump over the crack and break my mother's back, what the fuck happened?—I feel as though I've been assaulted. I know that sounds extreme, but I have been physically assaulted before, so I do know how that feels. I have said for years that what this illness has done is to make me punch drunk. I keep getting knocked down and I get up to be punched again. But I've *written* about this at length before; perhaps I need a different image for this thing that happens/is happening to my body.

I'm going to try and go for a walk. The sun looks like it's trying to come out. I will attempt to Walk in Beauty. I keep hoping that's the *key* but so far . . .

Before me, next to me, behind me, above and below me. Beauty, beauty, beauty.

Unfortunately Beauty's got bags under her eyes, her feet are sore, her nose is running, and her heart is aching. In all directions.

Blessed be.

NIGHT AT THE CASITA

January 29, 2005

Today was my last full day at the casita. I stayed here all day, writing. It rained part of the time while I wrote "Silver" in the Quail House. It was my last "mesquite" story. Usually I just made up a story and said it out loud as I sat under the mesquite tree. Today, for this last story here, I sat at the computer, wrote the tale, and then printed it out. Then I went and read it under the mesquite tree as the sun was going down.

"Silver" is based on the fairy tale of "Silver Hands." Something about this gruesome tale is familiar. It feels important, like some kind of key or answer to the riddle of my life. In the tale, Silver Hands goes into Nature and her hands start growing again. It is only then that she is reunited with her husband, the king, who is wandering the wilderness, unkempt and a little bit mad, in grief over the loss of his wife and son. Silver finds the animal-like man in the woods, recognizes him as her husband, and they are reunited and healed, as a family. Fairy tales are transformative. Stories are transformative. Terrible things happen to people in fairy tales—just as terrible things happen in real life. If a girl without hands can find a life again—can learn to care for herself and her family—who knows what could happen in our own lives?

After I finished reading my version out loud, I felt exuberant.

I laughed. I did a dance. I said goodbye and thank you to the desert. I felt like I flew back to the casita. Now I was ready to go home.

Later that night the moon was bright again, filling up the world. How many nights can it be full? The caretaker said she wasn't sure how many more days of a full moon her body could take. I laughed. I understood. Somehow time has stood still, giving us the space to be fully here. In full. Just like the full moon.

Earlier I saw a hawk fly to the tree on the south side of the house and look around for something good to eat (I presumed). As I finished reading "Silver," the owl called out. I went back to the casita to prepare dinner. The caretaker knocked on the door and said, "Kim, you've got to see this!" I ran into the house and we went outside (providing an opportunity for the dog to jump on me and bite my hand; no skin broken, thank you). In the east, a double rainbow arched in front of clouds that were all puffed up and black with storm. We laughed and danced around in the rain. It was cold and wet, so we didn't linger .

At one point as I was making dinner, I stopped and thought, "Oh, I have to hear the coyotes my last night." I stepped outside and they were howling, singing up a storm (almost literally). The clouds in the west caught the last rays of the sun, turning themselves scarlet. The coyotes stopped a few minutes later, so I was glad I had gone outside. When I was eating dinner, I thought, "Now I've just got to see the javelinas."

Soon after, the caretaker knocked again and I went into her part of the house, and then we went out her front door. It was still light out, and I could see a herd of javelinas digging around the front beds, about seven adults, with several little ones further away from the house. They were much bigger than I thought they'd be, black and hairy and as big as farm pigs. They didn't seem in the least concerned by us. A couple came up onto the porch where we were standing. The caretaker said they stank.

"Like what?" I asked. "Like pigs," she said. Two of the javelinas started having sex on the porch.

"So *that's* where little javelinas come from," I said.

Later, as I was typing up (and embellishing) another mesquite tale, Mario called from Portland. So tonight I had heard from the South (hawk), the East (rainbow and javelinas), the West (coyotes and the owl), and the North (Mario).

I thank all the directions, what is above and below. I thank this place, the Visibles, Invisibles, human, not human. It's been a time. Blessed be.

Thanks for listening.

Year Two

Church of the Old Mermaids

IN THE BURNING RING OF FIRE

January 6, 2006

Mario is reading *Shadow Cities,* and I'm sitting at the table listening to *Johnny Cash at Folsom Prison.* I grew up listening to Johnny Cash. Listened to my mother belt out "Burning Ring of Fire." I'd roll my eyes, but I enjoyed his songs. Mario and I went to see *Walk the Line* tonight. I was impressed. I never caught the leads acting, and the story was compelling. Had me crying and singing and wishing they were still alive. (Johnny Cash and his wife June Carter Cash died within months of each other in 2003.)

We're having a fine time in Tucson. I'm living the perfect life. I wake up next to my sweetheart. Eventually we get out of bed, have breakfast, then walk the wash or a trail at the park down the road. If we walk the wash, we stop by the Quail House first and turn on the heater and air purifier. After our walk, I go to the Quail House and write, and Mario goes back to the casita—the opposite of what we did last year. At lunch time, I return to the casita and Mario feeds me, usually beans and rice or a sandwich and soup. Then I go back to the Quail House and write some more.

Usually I take a break to walk the wash. The character in my novel walks the wash, too, so I'm usually walking for her or with her. I'm looking with my character's eyes as I walk. And she has found some astonishing and ordinary things: bottles, pieces of metal, pieces of plastic, an arrow, a shovel, and more. I've been putting what I find in the novel. It goes something like this:

> It was Saturday morning, and Myla walked the wash looking for trash in the dirt. She looked for treasure too. One man's trash was another woman's treasure. And vice versa. She always said. She carried two bags over her right shoulder. Into the plastic bag, she dropped garbage; into the ruby-colored cloth bag, she put those bits of refuse she thought she might sell on 4th Street, at the Church of the Old Mermaids. It was not a real church. At least not how most people defined "church." It was the space where she put her table, chair, and wares on Saturdays, shine or shine. She called it the Church of Old Mermaids because her mother told her when she was a child that the desert had once been a vast sea. She liked imagining that the mermaids had not dried up when the sea did; they merely changed their attitudes. And maybe their skin and fin-ware.
>
> Her feet slip-slided over the sand. A ground squirrel scurried out from beneath a paloverde whose bare green branches stretched out over the wash, dangling dry bean pods as though it wanted her to snatch up a couple. So she did. She dropped them into the ruby bag.
>
> "Thank you," she murmured. Wasn't about to say she wouldn't be able to get a nickel for them. Unless she came up with a particularly good story. Like how these pods came from the wash that used to be a river where the mermaids were stranded, when the sea be-

gan to dry; these pods came from a tree hanging over the wash where the mermaids were stranded, where they finally came to shore, and the first thing they did, these Old Mermaids, was to plant themselves a paloverde. All green, just like the Mother Star Stupendous Mermaid's tail had been, you know, before she had to leave the sea, the river, the wash.

Around 4:00, I go back to the casita. Then we walk again, or we sit and talk, or make dinner. Afterward we play games or read or go to a movie or a bookstore. They have a place here where you can see first run movies for three dollars. We also watched one season of *Upstairs, Downstairs* on my computer while playing cards and *Sorry*.

I'm very happy. I was sitting in the Quail House yesterday thinking, "I could do this the rest of my life."

I love my sweetie, love this place, love my book.

Love, love, love. Makes the world go 'round.

KEEP GOING

January 16, 2006

Tonight as we drove home, La Luna came up over the Rincons. Before the moon came up, we saw a strange light in the mountains we had not seen before. It was a rayed arc, red. Had an alien ship landed? More likely something exploded. No. That was too steady. The rayed arc was the "Ladies and Gentleman, Introducing . . . La Luna." As we neared home, the moon rose a bit so that it looked like the luminous eye of an alligator. We turned up the radio and drove on toward it. As we got closer to the mountains, the Moon slipped away again.

We've been listening to KXCI 91.3 FM. It's a community radio station and it broadcasts many genres of music. I've already bought far too many albums since we've been here because of this station. On the way to Mexico, as we drove down Highway 83 to Nogales, we heard a track from *Dust My Broom,* an album by Boozoo Bajou. I bought the album tonight, and the first track is "Keep Going" by Tony Joe White and Jody White. It's just someone giving directions, yet it is quite menacing.

The song begins, "You all ain't from around here, are you? Where you boys trying to git to? The swamp?. . . Go down a ways and you come to some crossroads. Keep going."

I turned it up loud. (I'm hoping our housemates at the other end of the house couldn't hear it.) Went outside and under that not quite full moon, I danced. A dog howled next door. A coyote yipped in the hills. And I danced. The horses ran around the corral. The stars above, oblivious, did the shimmy anyway.

Now it's time for bed. Was going to write some more but got distracted. I'm 55,000 words into the new novel. That's about 200 pages. I likes.

Friday night Mario and I walked the wash just about the time the Moon went full. Everything looked as though it had a layer of snow on it, but it was just moon milk. It was so light outside that we walked the wash where the coyotes, mountain lions (we're told), and bobcats (we're told) wander. Not sure I would have been wandering there at night had I known the last two lovelies walked this way.

I've been dreaming about cats since I've been here. We'd only been here a couple of nights before I dreamed two tigers killed Mario. The other night I dreamed a mountain lion and a jaguar were after me. Another night I dreamed Thomas Crow took me for a ride in his black helicopter. And John Goodman was playing Dr. Dude in the same sitcom where I was Roseanne's slutty sister; the stars made a cursive K in the sky just for me. In one dream, I was trying to communicate with this tiny frozen man; I knew he had something to say. I made him bigger and after much trouble he finally was able to say what he needed to say to me: "Shut up!" Last night I was in the service. Yep. Dark blue uniform and everything. It's a busy dream season.

No idea what any of it means. I'll just keep goin'.

FORK IN THE ROAD

January 26, 2006

We're leaving in a couple of days. Both feeling sad. We could do this the rest of our lives. Who couldn't? Virginia Woolf was right. A little money and room of one's own really does facilitate creativity. (If you haven't read it, "A Room of One's Own" is very inspiring. It is especially good read aloud.) This has been an absolutely lovely month. (Despite a skin condition that kept me up many nights and left me itchy and jumpy during the day.) I had Mario, this place, and my novel. Ahhh, bliss. We were quite compatible with our housemates as we went about our lives, separate, yet together under an umbrella of creativity.

I wrote and sold an essay, "Healing the Wounded Wild," the first week I was here. The next three weeks I worked on a novel, *Church of the Old Mermaids*. I finished the first draft last Friday. During that time, I also went to the jaguar conference, and I talked to conservationists, a biologist, ranchers, Mexicans, migrants, and others about border issues and jaguars (as separate and related issues).

We went to a trail where the migrants cross the desert and where some of them die. Last year when I was at this particular trail, a man with a gun came up to me and said, "Have you seen any illegals?" I guess he hadn't read the sign at the entrance to the trail: no guns. We said, "How would we know?" He said,

"I just rustled up about six of them." This day, we saw no other humans besides ourselves, but I found a great deal of evidence that others had passed this way, including a fork in the dust. The phrase "when you come to a fork in the road, take it" got stuck in my brain for a while.

La frontera—the border—is a complex place. Myla Alvarez, the hera of my novel, said of the border, "Thresholds. That was what it was. *La frontera* was a threshold. Like the wash. A betwixt and between place. Magic existed. Even though the magic was sometimes cruel and arbitrary."

Many of the things I believed when I first came here twenty years ago, I no longer believe. My kneejerk reaction that some people were bigots just because they were concerned about the traffic across the border was wrong. No one I've spoken with has expressed hatred for the migrants. In fact, everyone I've talked with has expressed sympathy or understanding for why they are trying to get here. Nearly everyone I've spoken with expressed frustration with the American and Mexican governments. The problems seem to get worse every time a politician decides to "fix it." Short-term fixes aren't working.

So what happens next?

THE OLD SEA

January 29, 2006

We've left Tucson and are now in a hotel in Valencia, California, just outside of Los Angeles. Close enough to the ocean to hear it. Almost. Mario is reading the paper right now. I've got the television on for the first time in six weeks. The Weather Channel. Interesting how I can step so easily out of one world and into another. Yes, it does feel like a different world. For six weeks, I have not been inundated with advertising and news. For six weeks, I have not received the ever present message "be afraid, be very afraid."

I finished the first draft of *Church of the Old Mermaids*. I wrote about thirty pages on Friday, January 19, and I figured I'd finish it the following day. But after dinner, I felt antsy, so I sat down at the desk in the casita and wrote the last scenes while Mario did the dishes. It was only about ten more pages.

I could hardly believe it. I had written nearly 80,000 words in three weeks (almost 300 pages). Fictional words. A novel. A story that dropped out of the clear blue sky or from the fingers of the old mesquite. Maybe it came to me from the empty wash. Of course, the wash is not really empty. It's filled with sand. Fairy sand, maybe. It got all over my shoes. My soles. Filled up my soul with fairy dust. Old Mermaid dust.

After I finished writing the book, I spent the rest of the week thanking the Universe for this story and this place where I came to remember it.

On Thursday, something seemed different in the wash and all around the house. Not different. That's not quite right. Hmmm. Maybe I was different. Something shifted. As if I could finally hear. Or see. I followed my instincts. Like following a child—a young girl—who still understands the trees, wind, rocks, birds. I followed coyote tracks and found seven sea shells in the dirt. *Sea shells in the desert.* I walked into the wash and saw a hummingbird at the top of a mesquite. I guess the hummingbirds in Arizona can sit still. Then it let go of the tree and flew right down toward me, all ruby-colored, shimmery, shiny, like Dorothy's shoes. Sometime later, I followed a roadrunner. After it disappeared beyond the horse corral, I looked down at its X marks the spot prints in the sand. Such mystery and truth in those lines.

Mario and I took our chairs and sat near where I had found the sea shells. We listened to the sun go down. I could not sit still for long. The wash was calling to me. Or something was. I walked down the left part of the Y, near the barn. Softly. Quietly. I stood at the crossroads of the Y, then walked back toward the house.

I went up near the house, out of the wash, and stood at the skeleton of the sweat lodge. I looked down at the stones in the middle. Thought about going inside but didn't. I stared at a splotch of bird shit that looked like a pictograph of a person, arms outstretched.

I wondered if I should stay out here all night to get a vision. Then I turned and walked a few steps, toward a picnic table. The setting sun light, golden, fell beneath the paloverde and mesquite that grew side by side near the front of the house, fell like a kind of twilight spotlight, or a wave of sweet light—that kind of light where you're certain anything can happen.

As I gazed at the place beneath the tree, something turned to me and opened her eyes. The sun had set in her eyes, golden red, split in two. She blinked and came into form. At first I thought she was a coyote. But her gaze was different. More fey. More direct. And her ears had tufts. Her face was rounder. I couldn't place what I was looking at. I put my hands together at my heart. "Oh," I said. And something else. Maybe, "stay"? I can't remember. She stood, sleepy, and I saw her whole body. I knew the form now. Saw her short tail. *Bobcat.* She was smaller than what I would have imagined. She walked away slowly, down into the wash and across, up into the desert. She looked back at me once. Then she was gone.

I looked for her. Looked for her prints in the old mermaid dust. It was enough I had seen her. Enough that she sat under the trees, next to the bench, close to the house. Enough that I asked for a vision, and she let me see her.

I went back to Mario. This trip has been filled with felines. The jaguar conference. My interviews with a conservationist and then a biologist about jaguars. Tigers, mountain lions, and jaguars had visited my dreams. Was it any wonder a bobcat appeared in waking life?

Later we had dinner and conversation with our new friends—the caretakers—after the owl called out.

On Friday, a week from when I finished the book, I took the items I had found in the wash, the ones I'd put in the book, and I assembled an Old Mermaid out of them. I called Mario over to help with the tail. We used palm fronds and prickly pear pads. We both got pricked several times.

When she appeared to be finished, I thanked the spirits and beings of the place, I thanked the Old Mermaids, I thanked everything and everyone, and offered the art piece as a gift. I poured out water in the four directions.

So much feels healed from this trip. I feel different. I don't think I feel like the Furious Spinner (the name of my original blog) any more, at least not in the same way. I'm not so angry. I feel more like an Old Mermaid, learning to swim in the ocean of my being, in the old sea that is this world. I am a novice in the Church of the Old Mermaids. I found solace and peace at the Old Mermaids Sanctuary for thirty-eight days. I want to carry that solace and peace with me. The Old Mermaids solve problems differently than I do. I want to learn from them. And that bobcat. She was invisible until she opened her eyes. She was invisible until she turned and looked at me. But she wasn't, was she? When I saw her, she saw me. *I saw the wild looking at me.* It sounds like a song, doesn't it? One I could sing for the rest of my life.

Today, as we left the Old Mermaids Sanctuary, a coyote walked by our car. Just like last year: at the last minute, Coyote said hello and goodbye. We thanked him and went on our way.

The journey continues.

Year Three

Old Mermaids Sanctuary

RABIES, BABIES

January 6, 2007

We went down to Saguaro National Park for a quick hike before starting our work for the day. It was our first time there this season, and we were greeted with a sign that read: RABIES. We were cautioned that "there were indications" rabies was present in the park, and we should watch out for it. Bobcats, foxes, and raccoons especially could get quite aggressive when they had rabies. Mario started laughing and said, "Remember last year they had a mug shot of a mountain lion?" And the year before that they warned us about killer bees. Good times.

Then we came home and I went out to the Quail House to write. I stalled for an inordinate amount of time. I couldn't find my red pen so I looked for it. Stalling. Went to check the mail. Stalling. Checked the path to the mail for my red pen. More stalling. Took photographs of my work area. Stall, stall, big stall. Hugged an old mesquite. Priceless. (Sorry.)

About 3:30 p.m. I decided to call it a day. I picked up my laptop, manuscript, and camera and opened the door. Out of the corner of my vision I saw a creature moving away, startled by me opening the door. I turned to look at it. Bobcat! She was back. (Or another one was. Remember last year I had an encounter with a bobcat on my last day here.) The bobcat did not seem to be in any hurry. She kept stopping to look back at me, as if to say, "What are you waiting for? You asked for an adventure and here I am ready to take you." I put my computer down in the wash, in the dirt, and I followed her.

At one point, I squatted to take photographs. (I asked her if it was all right; not sure what her answer was, but she didn't run away.) Mario hadn't gotten to see the bobcat last year, so I decided to go into the casita and get him. When we came back into the wash, the bobcat was gone, but we did find her prints in the sand.

At no point during our encounter was I frightened even though a little voice in my head kept screaming, "Rabies!"

And I replied, "Did you say babies?"

Not a bad day.

SONGS OF THE SPIRIT

January 10, 2007

I am listening to *Songs of the Spirit* while Mario does the dishes. I just finished sweeping and mopping. I sweep every day and mop every few days. I like sweeping these stone floors; I like watching the stone change as I press the wet mop down on them. It's raining. The sound mixes with *Songs of the Spirit*. This is the music that was playing when I went in for my surgery; it was what was playing while they operated on me, while I was awake and while I was asleep.

I am in the desert. It usually takes about a week for me to settle in, and it's been a bit over a week. Mario has finished writing one novel and started another. I wrote an Old Mermaid story, and today I started a new novel. It is tentatively called *The Old Mermaids School of Telling Tales and Finding Art*. Mostly, I've been enjoying the place and getting used to things. At first the noise always troubles me. I can hear the traffic, they're doing construction, dogs bark, and trail bikes whine in the near distance. When I go into the Quail House or into the casita those sounds usually disappear, but I want to be in desert, in the wash. I want to hear the birds. I want to hear the silence.

Eventually, I know the other sounds won't matter. (Unless the trail bikes get closer; if they do, that is a noise I cannot tolerate.) I know what time the dogs usually bark (around 5:00), and the construction is intermittent and can become a dull background noise. And I know I only notice these sounds because it is quiet, and eventually I will get to hear the desert silence. It is different from any other silence. How to explain it? It is desolate and comforting. And when you hear the sound of another creature, it's as if you're all in it together—you're all in this place surviving and thriving and figuring it out as *compañeros*.

Today I had one of those silent desert days. I walked the wash and walked the wash, just like Myla, looking for trash I could turn into treasure. I figured out what I was going to write next and listened to my feet crunching over the sand. Quail walked daintily, all in a row, up and out of the wash. Doves fluttered from the trees as I went by, startling me and them. Then I sat outside near the Quail House. I listened to the whoosh-whoosh-whoosh as a crow flew overhead. I heard the owl call out twice. Thrashers and other birds made themselves known. Desert cottontails hopped here and there and everywhere. Once in a while I heard the horses snort or whinny. Clouds moved overhead, putting me in and out of shade. Nothing could have been grander.

Before that, I was restless most of the day, moving from here to there and everywhere. Mario said it's what I do before I start a novel; it's the creative energy rising up. I wrote the first 1,000 words of the novel today. It was nice to be with Myla and Lily again, but it was a bit nerve-wracking. I've never written a book using the same characters from another book I've written.

Now we're getting ready for sleep. I'm listening to Linda Rondstadt and Ann Savoy's *Adieu False Heart*. I think they call it Cajun folk, and it is so beautiful, my heart aches as I listen. I have never been able to describe music. When it's right, when it's beautiful, it is beyond words. Maybe most beauty is that way—or should be.

THE PINK SHOE

January 13, 2007

Today Mario and I attended the Borders Issues Fair put on by the Santa Cruz Valley Border Issues Coalition. This was the third year of this fair, and it was held in Green Valley, which is about an hour from where we're living. People were there from Borderlinks, No More Deaths, Las Madras Project, Just Coffee, Humane Borders, Samaritans, and other organizations—most of them faith-based. The large meeting room was filled with hundreds of people, most of them over sixty, most of them middle-class Anglos. Mario and I spent the day in their company being amazed, inspired—and sometimes teary-eyed.

The speakers were all good. Those who lived in *la frontera*, in the region near the border, said they felt as though they were in a "low-intensity war." Black hawk helicopters and the Border Patrols were a daily part of their lives. They could be stopped at any time, and they were, on the pretext of national security, and they had to show ID. The Border Patrol, and now the local police who were helping them, were often belligerent with members of this community when they asked for ID. (These are American citizens, by the way, living right here in Arizona.)

The speakers talked about the root causes of illegal immigration. They talked about global economics and "savage capitalism" which devastates communities. (Multi-global corporations, dumping of products, etc.) The Reverend Delle McCormick gave statistics about the poverty in Mexico. The Reverend Mark Adams talked about the coffee cooperative he and others started on the borderlands. Joseph Nevins gave a historical prospective on immigration and immigration laws in the United States over time.

Joseph Nevins talked about mobility being a basic human right. He said, "Security in the United States is a 'god' word, something universally embraced and insufficiently questioned." Despite the billions of dollars that have been spent on border "security," just as many people get into this country illegally as did before they spent billions of dollars. (Reverend Mark Adams said they lent the coffee cooperative $20,000, and now that cooperative is supporting 37 families. Imagine what could have been done with all those billions of dollars the government had spent on security. If people can feed their families, they don't want to leave their own lands.)

Nevins said, "Despite a massive build up in resources, drugs and migrants still cross. About one-third get caught. 92 to 97% eventually succeed. There's no difference between before and after the buildup at the border.... Political actors have exaggerated the security threat. They say there haven't been any attacks since 9/11, but there weren't any attacks the five years before 9/11 when they had spent much less." (Did you know 25% of the prisoners in the world are in our jails, even though we have 5% of the world's population?)

Nevins said we need to change the language of the debate on this issue. He pointed out that the Minutemen are using the deaths in the borderlands as a reason to have increased border security. Nevins said we need to say that we don't want any more deaths, and we are interested in basic human rights, which include the right to mobility and the reunification of families.

Later when I went to the Samaritans table and saw all the items they had picked up from the desert, dropped by passing migrants, I started to cry. The woman standing next to me said, "Seeing this kind of gets to you, doesn't it?" I thought of Myla walking the wash and picking up what she found there and taking it to the Church of the Old Mermaids. I thought of her walking the desert near *la frontera* and finding Lily, left there as though she was trash. Myla said, "Lily held out her arms to me, and I embraced her. From that second on, I knew I would lay down my life for her; it was as though I had given birth to her—or she to me." I wish every one of those people who walked the desert had had someone like Myla. I wish they didn't have to walk the desert. I wish they could walk into this country with dignity and return to their own countries when they wished with dignity.

The stories about the people who have crossed were very powerful. Mark Adams talked about the man who said how painful it was to leave his land. Joseph Nevins talked about the thirteen-year-old boy who dragged his mother's body across the desert for days after she died from heat exhaustion. He talked about Olivia Luna who was only eleven years old when she was found on Tohono O'odham land. They found Olivia Luna in the desert dying, he said, wearing pink sneakers. I gasped (yes, really, out loud) when he said this. I glanced at Mario; he looked stunned, too.

I had started my new Old Mermaids book this week. In the first scene, Lily and Myla are walking the wash together looking for things to take to the Church of the Old Mermaids. They aren't finding anything until:

A desert cottontail scurried across the wash in front of them, slipping on the loose dirt and looking completely panicked before it jumped up out of the arroyo. Lily clapped. Myla noticed something in the sand near where the rabbit had made its getaway. She and Lily walked over to it.

A tiny bit of pink stuck up out of the sand. Myla bent down. The rabbit's scrambling must have exposed it. Lily crouched next to her. Myla began pushing away the dirt with her cotton-gloved fingers. It was the heel end of a pink shoe.

All week I've been saying to Mario, "I know I'm going to find a pink shoe somewhere."

And there it was, on the foot of Olivia Luna Noguera.

That's the way writing these books and stories has worked. Recently I started to lose faith in what I was doing. How could me telling stories, particularly stories of the Old Mermaids, be accomplishing anything, even though they meant so much to me? As I thought about Olivia and all her companion walkers, I realized again that the Old Mermaids had walked up onto these shores, this New Desert, without shoes, without anything, because their home had dried up (literally). They were migrants; we are all migrants, every day, trying to find our way in this land and in our lives. *Church of the Old Mermaids* was always about migrants coming together to create community.

I want to tell the stories of people like precious Olivia Luna. I want to tell the story of every item I see on that table, just as Myla told stories of what she found in the wash. I want to find the truth in those stories. And I'm hoping telling these tales will in some way contribute, in some way document what is happening—maybe even transform it on some level. Who knows?

I wish I had been in that desert to hold my arms out to Olivia Luna the day she tried to cross the desert. I would have wiped her tears and tied the shoelaces of her pink tennis shoes. I would have protected her, no matter what.

At least I'd like to think so.

On Monday, I spoke with two women who volunteer for Humane Borders. Elizabeth and Audrey very kindly told me how a group of people from various walks of life with many different faith traditions decided they wanted to help prevent migrant deaths as they traversed the Arizona desert. How best to do that? Most of the fatalities were caused by dehydration, so the volunteers who were a part of Humane Borders decided to put water out in the desert for the migrants. There are now more than eighty watering stations on this side of the border (and they donated some for the other side of the border, too). Each station is marked with a blue flag.

It seems like such a simple idea, doesn't it? Sometimes I think there is no way to fix all the problems in the world. We've got to do this, that, and the other. I remember someone telling me once that if everyone did just one thing, really devoted time and energy to one thing, then eventually all the things would get fixed. The people at Humane Borders are holding out water to thirsty people. That is their one thing. I love the elegance of this solution. When someone is dying of thirst in the desert, I doubt they are thinking about international politics or how to fix global economics. They don't need that. They need water.

Of course, actually putting up and then maintaining these water stations isn't exactly simple. They need to keep the barrels filled with water, replace ones that are stolen or damaged, and regularly pick up litter and replace first aid kits and emergency rations at the water stations.

I admire these people, for their solution, their efforts, and their great kindness.

BRIDGES

January 19, 2007

This morning we awakened to rain. We went out into a glorious cool morning, and I could smell the rain. Or I could smell the desert after a rain. What a miracle it was to be able to smell. And there is nothing like the desert after a rain. Everything is plump and juicy and ecstatic. I told Mario it's like being in a world where everyone and everything got lucky the night before.

We headed down to Nogales, Mexico, to go to the No More Deaths tent just across the border. Part of the reason I wanted to do this was for research for my novel which is now called *Old Mermaids Sanctuary*. But immigration is also an issue I have been interested in and involved with (on the periphery) for many years.

Part of what I want to do with both *Church of the Old Mermaids* and *Old Mermaids Sanctuary* is to tell migrant stories. My husband is an immigrant. Both his parents endured great hardship to leave their countries in hopes of a better life. Nearly all of us who live in this country are here because an ancestor left his or her country to come here.

With all of this in mind, we headed down south. I had gotten directions from two people who volunteered with No More Deaths. They both told me that Gilberto would be at the tent, and he knew English and he could answer any questions I had.

We got a little lost on our way down, but eventually we came to what looked like a truck stop. I saw concrete blocks which was where Shura had told me to park. In the parking lot men stood around, watching and waiting—I don't know what they were waiting for; they just had that air. Several of them were on cell phones. Shura had told me to park the car and then walk toward the chain link fence. I saw chain link fences everywhere. And there were semi trucks everywhere lined up to go through one gate. I'm sure there was some kind of order to it all, but it seemed like chaos to me. The air pulsed with the sound of these trucks. The wind was blowing. It was cold. If we walked to where the trucks were going, I couldn't see that we'd end up anywhere. I couldn't see a pedestrian entrance. It was like being in a very confusing noisy industrial park. We didn't know where to go or what to do.

Finally I asked a man who was walking by how we could get into Mexico. He didn't speak English. So I asked a woman. She thought I wanted to be on the U.S. side, but I told her I was going to the tent on the other side, the No More Deaths tent. She seemed to think that was a bit strange (or I was), but in her accented English she kindly told me where to go. I thanked her, and then as I kept walking, we became separated by an orange fence. She smiled at me, and I smiled at her, and we both shrugged at the divide and went our separate ways. There was something sad and poignant about our separation that I can't really explain, except that I know we both felt it; I saw it in her eyes as the bars came between us.

Mario and I went through the turnstile, and then we were in Mexico. It's always amazing to me all the fuss there is to get into this country and absolutely no fuss to go into Mexico. Two lanes of road were backed up from as far as I could see with cars waiting to get into the United States. The sun reflected off the tops of the cars, and I couldn't look at them. The road going into Mexico was empty. Concrete blocks were everywhere, it seemed, trying to keep something out, making it barely a road. Mario and I couldn't figure out where to go.

In the near distance I saw a big building. Shura had told me to look for the customs building, so Mario and I walked toward that, weaving in and out of moving cars and people. We crossed the road and walked past a long line of men. When we reached the building, I saw the No More Deaths tent.

As we got near the small white tent with a small trailer next to it, two Anglo women inside turned toward us. One said, "Are you Kim?" I said that I was. I went toward them and introduced myself and Mario. In the back of the tent, a man stood by the stove cooking. I asked if he was Gilberto. He said that he was. I asked him if Shura had told him who I was and what I was doing. I repeated that I was a writer and I wanted to ask some questions if that was all right with everyone, and I told him I could help out, too.

The tent was open on one end, closed where Gilberto stood by the stove. The dirt floor was wet and muddy. Behind Gilberto was a mound of clothes; I assumed those were extra clothes for the migrants. On the south side of the narrow tent, four migrants sat: three women and one man. A cot near the opening of the tent had a wet sleeping bag on it. On the north side of the tent was a table with a mishmash of supplies on it: food, water, paper towels, cutlery, etc. Near the opening of the tent were the first aid supplies. The two volunteers for No More Deaths were organizing the supplies.

I squatted next to the migrants and asked if they spoke English. None of them did. I asked Gilberto if he would mind translating. He agreed to do that.

And so I began speaking with Alicia, Theresa, Phillipe, and Caterina. Alicia and Theresa were very shy. Theresa kept her hand over her mouth most of the time, even when she spoke softly. Caterina and Phillipe were brother and sister, and they talked with me the most. I asked them all if they had been treated well when they were picked up by *la migra*. They said they had been. They were given crackers and water, and no one was hurt. I asked them why they had tried to cross illegally. They said they wanted "a better life for my family." I asked if there weren't job where they lived. Phillipe said there were jobs, but the pay was bad. They said they could make only about $4 a day.

The four migrants had each left children behind, thirteen in all. They felt they had to do this so that they could come to America and make money. They all said they wanted to stay only a few months, make some money, and then return home. Gilberto said, "When they get to the other side, the *chollos* are waiting for them. They have guns and they rob them." I asked if the chollos—gangsters, he said—were Americans or Mexicans. "Oh no," he said. "They are Mexicans. Sometimes they make the women take off all her clothes and they see if she's hiding anything up there. Sometimes they rape the women. One man came in here, tears coming down his face, and he say they raped his wife. Fifteen years old." I said that was very sad. (Understatement of the year, but that's about all I knew how to say in Spanish.) They all agreed if was very *triste*.

I had Gilberto ask the migrants if they had just been robbed by chollos. They had been. Phillipe described with his hands that they had taken the money in his wallet, his ring, the chain around his neck. He said there was nothing he could do because they put a gun to his head.

I asked Gilberto why the *guia*—the coyote—didn't take the migrants on a different route if the chollos waited in the same spot all the time. He said the coyotes were in on it. When the chollos robbed the migrants, they always asked, "Who is the guia? Then they take him aside. They don't rob him." I asked if they could cross without a guide. They said no. They needed someone else on the other side to pick them up, and the guia knew the way through the desert.

I asked if the desert trek was very difficult. Phillipe said to get across it was about eighteen hours, but it wasn't too bad. He said they saw coyotes, the canine kind, and the Border Patrol told them there was a mountain lion up by Tucson. I asked Gilberto if the Border Patrol was telling the truth or just trying to scare them. He said they were trying to "make them afraid."

I asked if crossing was different now from what it used to be. They all said it was much more dangerous. They said it would be easier if they could just come across and work and then go home again.

I asked Gilberto if he knew of women with children at home and without husbands who were crossing. (He didn't know what I meant when I asked about single women. I have heard that thousands of single mothers live in this country, work, and send money back home to children they may not see for years.) He said he did know of some women like that. "But they shouldn't do it. No, they should stay home."

The other volunteers left, and Mario and I helped prepare a meal. Mario cut up tomatoes and onions for *huevos* that Gilberto was making. More people came into the tent. I helped get coffee. A man came in who was very hungry. He quickly ate several tortillas and beans. Gilberto made the huevos (scrambled eggs, tomatoes, onions), and then Mario and I served the migrants. We gave them all forks, which was silly. They just wrapped the huevos up in the tortillas and ate them that way.

After everyone had eaten, Mario and I decided it was time to go. I shook hands with everyone and thanked them. They thanked me, too. Caterina put her hand over mine and said something very kind, but I didn't know what. (I understood some of what they were saying, even though my Spanish is twenty years gone.) I asked Gilberto to ask them to all be careful. He repeated what I said in Spanish, and everyone in the tent responded to that. They looked at us and nodded, said *gracias*.

Then we left. We made our way through the concrete jungle back toward the turnstile. Cars, cars, cars everywhere. I couldn't really digest any of it because it was so overstimulating—I just concentrated on not getting hit by any vehicles. Finally we approached a single guard who asked us what our citizenship was. And then we went through the turnstile again, crossed another street, and got into our car.

Before we went home, we decided to go to the tourist part of Nogales. We got back on 19 and drove to the end, parked by the Burger King, and walked to Mexico. This entrance was much quieter, less cacophonous. I wanted to see again the white crosses on the border fence; each one represented a migrant who had died trying to cross the border.

I also wanted to buy something. If my dollars could help a family that was trying to live on $4 a day, I wanted to do that. We walked down the streets and responded as the various barkers tried to get us to go into their stores. I enjoy the banter. When I do go into a store, I'm always amazed that they all seem to think we are rich. Today I realized that if someone is trying to live on $4 a day, we are rich, no matter what we may think.

I bought a rattle, box, and ceramic cat for the woman who is taking care of our house, all for $13. We got a ceramic sun from another shop. After we bought it, we stood outside talking to the man next to a huge pile of cow skulls. Georgia O'Keeffe would have loved it. He told us that after it rained, like today, and the sun came out, the skulls would really start to stink. I said, "That's a lot of dead cows." Steers, I guess they were, because they had horns. He said they're from slaughterhouses. The skulls are put out into the desert until they're just bone.

Later we stopped by a shop that had beautiful finely woven rugs. I was admiring these works of art and letting the man show me rug after rug when I realized that I was wasting his time. He was trying to make a living, and I was looking at rugs I could not afford. We did buy a red kokopelli blanket from him, however.

By this time, we were exhausted. Most Americans are not accustomed to this kind of shopping, including us. And I am not accustomed to shopping at all. We left Nogales and headed home. Soon after we got on the freeway, a golden eagle came straight for our car but veered off just before I hit it. I had to actually brake on an expressway to keep from hitting the eagle.

About thirty miles up the road, we had to stop at a checkpoint. The Border Patrol was set up under Agua Linda Road. As our car neared where the officer was, I got angrier and angrier. *What has happened to our country? How have we let ourselves come to this? This is the United States of freaking America and I was being subjected to a police search without cause, without notice, without reason. It is outrageous.* The blond boy looked at our lily white faces and waved us past.

Mario patted my leg and said, "It's all right."

"It's not all right," I said. "It's really not all right. We're just lucky we look like what their version of an American is."

Once we neared Tucson, the drive got tedious. Too many long desert roads with too many cars and too many lights. We were exhausted. Then we saw a storm over the Catalinas. And the light. And the clouds. We opened the window and breathed deeply. The Rincon Mountains weren't visible, covered in storm clouds or dusk or mystery.

We followed the rainbow home. Drove right over it as though it were a bridge. How easy it was for us.

I wish the world had more bridges and less walls and fences.

Wouldn't that be grand?

WHO?

January 20, 2007

I'm waiting for the eggs to set before I continue making breakfast. I just did the dishes. Mario is writing. It's a cloudy cool day. I didn't wake up to the owl this morning. I said to Mario, "I've been deserted by my lover." He said, "It's a myth that they're wise." I laughed.

It's always good to wake up laughing.

Here's the thing about the owl: The first year we were here, we heard the owl in the palm tree behind the casita every night and every morning. But it was warmer that year, and we had the door open pretty much all the time. Last year we didn't hear her/him as much. Both years it seemed as though some lovin' was going on between two owls in the palm tree. As I said last year, don't come a knockin' when the palm tree's a rockin'.

But this year I forgot it was mating season. The other night ,I heard the owl near dusk and I went to look for it in the palm tree. (Since I don't know if it's a he or a she, I'm going to call it 'it' and hope it doesn't mind.) Mario came out and looked with me. I tried to hoot back at the owl, but I didn't have the sequence quite right. Mario had figured it out, though, so he demonstrated softly how it would go. "Who-whooo who who." So I looked up at the tree and said, "Who-whooo who who." A second later the owl flew right down at us—and then over our heads and away. I figured it was a coincidence, but Mario thought the owl's action was in direct response to whatever I had said in owl language.

The next night when the owl woke up and began who-whooing again, I went out and spoke with it. I varied my who-whoo a bit in emphasis, but I stuck to the sequence. The owl responded about four seconds after I called out to it, every time. If I didn't say anything, the owl didn't say anything. This went on for a while, and then an owl flew away—but the owl I was talking to kept talking to me. I was appalled. I had thought there was only one owl in the tree. What if I had interfered with their mating ritual? ("Home wrecker," Mario said.) The other owl decided she/he couldn't compete with me? Or was annoyed by me? *Hasta la vista, baby.*

I went back into the house right away, figuring I had interfered enough.

And this morning we heard nary a who.

Ah well.

Birds keep diving at us during this trip. The owl, the golden eagle, other smaller birds.

What's it all about, Alfie?

The eggs are ready. Oh, ick. I just realized what I am about to eat.

At least they're not owl eggs.

Year Four

The Blue Tail

TAKING CARE

January 2, 2008

It's night at the Old Mermaid Sanctuary. A strong wind rattles the dry leaves in the palm tree just outside our door. The great horned owl is long gone, I'd imagine, out hunting. I haven't heard any coyotes. No animal sounds of any kind. Just the wind in the palm tree. And then silence. Profound, dark silence.

It's been a time. I still feel so unmoored. (My mother died unexpectedly four weeks ago.) I'm having excruciating back pain. This morning, I felt this spasm in my side. It was as though a muscle decided to pull one of my ribs out of place. I was in tears—and in agony. After I put hot towels on it and took a hot shower and then a hot bath, Mario and I went into the desert and walked for about an hour. We also talked. Mario believes the backache is psychological in nature. I wondered if it was from a too soft bed or from driving 15 hours the day before.

Mario pointed out that I always feel as though I have to fix things. I can't bring my mother back, and I can't help my father. I can't make anything better right now—I can't FIX anything.

And I keep thinking about everything I'm doing wrong. When I was in Santa Cruz to see my father and sister and her husband, we went to the Forest of Nisene Marks, where I'd been several years earlier. I wanted to show my father the redwoods there. I found out my father had not eaten since early in the morning, and now it was about seven hours later. My father has to eat something every two or three hours or his blood sugar drops (or something) and he gets depressed and has other symptoms. He's just getting over an illness (shingles) and he's still reeling from my mother's death. Right now I feel like he needs someone to watch over him, just like any person would under these circumstances no matter what their age. Anyway, I was chastising my brother-in-law for not making sure my father ate, and my father was getting a little annoyed with me. I realized later that I was probably sounding like one of those adult children who treats their parent like a child. I didn't mean to do that, and I keep worrying over these kinds of things.

I feel as though I am failing at everything. I know this is wrong thinking.

Ten minutes before my back went into spasm, I was in bed looking up at the ceiling and wishing I could stay here forever. And then one of the many little voices in my leetle brain said, "Bad things can happen here too."

Well, of course they can! Tucson is where I developed allergies and asthma and where my whole life went into a terrible downward spin for so many years. . . .

Anyway, soon after that my father called and soon after that, my back spasmed.

By the way, in the middle of the redwoods, away from the ocean, mind you, I discovered two seashells. Near this huge old redwood off the trail. I thought they were mushrooms at first, but then I saw they weren't. I said, "Dad, look. The Old Mermaids have been here. Remember from the book, if you find a seashell away from the ocean it means a mermaid just found her tail." Near to it was a circle. Perhaps someone left the shells as offerings.

Did they pray to an Old Mermaid? Does this mean I'm the Old Mermaid who heard their prayers?

I wish you happiness, good health, and much love.

Today I sat by the pool, the beautiful curving pool that has an Old Mermaid painted in the bottom of it . . . at least it does in my imagination and in *Church of the Old Mermaids*. The old owl slept in the palm tree above me, buffeted but seemingly unmoved by the winds.

Across from me was a statue of part of a woman. Ordinarily I love the art here. There is something new every year. This partial woman turned up last year. She has no legs or hands. I don't like this. I'm not saying it's bad art; I'm only saying I don't like it. I don't like art of dismembered people. Never have

Every time I look at this partial woman thing, I think of violence and helplessness. I want to run over and reattach her hands—which are on the ground near her—and fashion her new legs and tell her to run, run, run to safety. I see this place as a healing sanctuary, and the dismembered woman doesn't fit with that. There are also heads in my enclosed garden this year. Four of them. Quite gruesome. I want them gone. Every time I step outside, I have to avert my eyes. It's not restful or healing. Will I grow accustomed to them? Last year I didn't go out to the pool side much. I couldn't stand seeing the dismembered woman. Today I just stared at her.

We got here in the dark. The headlights of the car lit up the shovel I'd found in the wash so many years ago, the shovel that became the tail of an Old Mermaid, in real life and in the novel.

I'm so tired and sad. I feel stingy. There is so much I have. I remember the quote by e. e. cummings, probably because I've read it here somewhere at the Old Mermaid Sanctuary: "I thank you God for this most amazing day, for the leaping greenly spirits of trees, and for the blue dream of sky and for everything which is natural, which is infinite, which is yes."

I had more to say. But my back is aching. Everything is aching. Maybe I'll read for a bit. Or just close my eyes. Perhaps I'll dream. The Old Mermaids will come into my dreams and take care of me.

Maybe one of the Old Mermaids will be my mother.

Six hours later

Awaken from a dream. It's long and complicated, but in the end, I'm in a car that my mother is driving. I'm in the back. My father sits next to her. I ask her a question, and she can't remember the answer. She pulls the car over and says there are so many things she doesn't remember. She looks at me and then hugs my father. "Tell Kim it'll be all right," she says.

I awaken. It takes a long time to go back to sleep. I take another bath to alleviate the pain in my back. I'm so exhausted I can't think or feel. I nearly fall asleep in the hot water.

Morning

The rash on my hands has started. Sometimes I wonder why I come here every year. The first year I had a bad rash on my back, plus there was an obnoxious dog here which kept me confined to certain parts of the property, and I got pricked by nearly every cactus on the property. The second year I had another rash, but I also wrote *Church of the Old Mermaids*. Last year I remembered to bring white cotton gloves, so I didn't get a rash. And I wrote another novel, *The Old Mermaid Sanctuary*. Now I've got a backache and a rash. And there are human heads growing in my garden. When I'm here for a month, these nuisances fade. Since I'll be here less than two weeks this time, I wonder if I'll have time to acclimate.

Still, the Old Owl is here, quails flutter as we walk the property, and I found bobcat prints in the wash. Magic awaits. I know it. Or I used to know it. We'll see.

NIGHT AT THE OLD MERMAID SANCTUARY

January 12, 2008
I'm sitting in the casita listening to the blues. Love me those blues, darlin's. It is dark out, and we've spent most of the evening getting ready to leave tomorrow.

Yep, we'll soon be on our way back to the Pacific Northwest. I wish we could stay here longer, but I'm also looking forward to going home. I've been on the road so much since October that I'm ready to be home. I want to lounge on my couch (which is really a very old futon and not very comfortable) and eat bonbons. I actually don't know what a bonbon is, besides a "good good," so I'll just sit on my couch and eat something good good.

I want to go to Powell's Books. I went to Barnes & Noble, Borders, and Antigone at least twice each while here, and I couldn't find anything I wanted. I'd stand in these stores and look around and think, "There are no answers here."

I felt like a zombie for the first part of our visit here. I told you about my back, which did get better after I took the caretaker's suggestion to remove the "cushion" to make the bed harder. Isn't it interesting how a hard bed gives some people backaches and a soft bed gives other people backaches?

This year two great horned owls hung out in the palm tree

near the casita. Did I tell you this already? We woke up to their calls every morning and listened to them wake up and prepare for the hunt every evening. The first few days here, I sat out by the pool with my old mermaid quilt. I walked the wash, too. Every day, Mario and I walked to Saguaro National Park and hiked it a bit.

I never saw the bobcat. We did see coyotes several times. One day at dusk we saw two very large coyotes in the wash. I decided to follow them. Sometimes I'm not too bright. I have such an affinity for coyotes that I sometimes forget they are canines and might not want some little human trailing them. Anyway, we stopped at the fork in the wash and hid in plain sight by an old paloverde, hoping the coyotes would just walk right by us. After a minute or two, we heard this deep, low, guttural sound. We both got chills. Hair stood up on the back of my neck.

I said, "That's the javelinas. They've come out for the night." I remembered when I saw them four winters ago, they made a snorting sound; I figured this had to be the same thing. Though really, the sound we were hearing now was freaky scary, like something out of a horror movie, so I was just talking to reassure myself. The noise didn't stop, and I thought, "That can't be the javelinas."

I stepped into the wash to see if I could see anything. Just then a dog started to bark. I realized the sound we had heard was a growl, which was exactly what it sounded like. The dog barked and barked.

Mario said, "Well, that's gonna scare away the coyotes."

I yelled, "Shut up!"

The dog kept barking. We looked around and couldn't see this dog even though it sounded like it was only a few feet away from us. Dusk was threatening to turn to darkness. "Shut up, shut up, shut up!" I yelled. And suddenly the bark turned into a "yip-yip-yippppp." It was a coyote!

I had told a coyote to shut up. Geez Louise.

I immediately apologized to the wild thing. The coyote did not stop barking or yipping. Mario and I decided we must have violated some kind of unknown (to us) territory agreement. We were allowed the wash in the daytime, but at dusk it belonged to the wild things.

We went back to the house and sat on the porch. The coyote continued to bark, alone. I kept apologizing to it. I said I was sorry I had told it to shut up (and secretly promised not to tell dogs to shut up any more). I encouraged it to let its voice be heard.

As we sat on the porch in the dark, the barking continued and seemed to get closer. It was rather unnerving, the whole thing. I'm not sure why. Maybe because I had so misjudged the situation—and I still didn't know what was going on.

The coyote continued barking until our housemates came home.

A couple of nights we waited under the palm tree to watch the owls take off for the evening. It was great fun. The owls watched us too. I waved. Did you ever notice how owls act a lot like cats? The way they look at people. The way they move their heads from side to side.

And then some days I was so filled with regret and grief about my mom that I didn't know what to do with myself.

So I ate too much. I wondered if I would just keep eating until I was the size of two people, then three, then more. I'd carry around my sadness as extra weight, unexpressed, unfelt.

One day we were driving toward an art gallery/chapel on the north side of Tucson, toward the Catalinas. I stared at these beautiful mountains and felt such awe and love for them. On the radio, Paul Carrack was singing "The Living Years," and tears started flowing down my face. I wanted more than anything just to fall to my knees on the sweet hard earth and curl into a ball.

Thinking about touching the earth made me feel better. What I want to do with my life is to be able to stand my ground no matter what happens in my life. I want to be able to face life, look at it, know what it is, and not pretend it is something else.

Mario and I walked in the desert a lot these past two weeks. We talked about life, work, love, and death. We talked about how, in our view, the Universe is neutral to us and our existence. I didn't believe some omniscient being was out there looking down (or up) at me ready to help me, save me, or destroy me. And the randomness or the meaninglessness of death and life . . . made me wonder about everything. What was the sense of doing anything? We're all going to die.

We're all going to become nothing.

That's very disconcerting.

One day, I drove up to Scottsdale to spend a couple of days with my family. It was great to see my Dad. He looked good, his shingles all gone, just a little black eye. We spent the day walking around. Later we had dinner over at my other sister's place next door to my dad's townhouse. Afterward we watched Eddie Izzard's *Dress to Kill* (again) and I laughed so hard it hurt. When we went back to my dad's townhouse, I was standing in the kitchen when I saw my dad spray something into the hepa fan. I thought it was some kind of air freshener, but I haven't been able to smell anything in about three weeks so I couldn't tell. Just then my brother-in-law came in and said, "Is that pesticides?" It sounded like he was kidding. And then I realized my father was spraying pesticides into a fan that was then dispersing it into the air. And he was spraying it near my phone and purse and all of my things.

I couldn't believe it.

I said, "Dad, is that a pesticide?"

He didn't say anything. I said, "Fuck, Dad. That stuff makes me sick."

You know how you go into those states of total disbelief and utter fear and panic all at the same time? That's what happened to me. Anyone who knows even a tiny bit about me knows that I'm pesticide sensitive and I've been working to eliminate (or reduce) the use of pesticides pretty much everywhere. I don't travel without finding out if the hotels use pesticides. I don't go any place where I know they've used pesticides. And here my father had these poisons in his house and was using them.

I couldn't believe he had done that. And I immediately fell back into my paranoid mode of "my family doesn't understand me." I went outside. I was so angry and hurt. I can't articulate how upset I was. I didn't know if I was going to have an asthma attack. I didn't know what was going to happen to me. I didn't know if I'd have to throw out all my stuff—including a brand new phone and my computer.

I said to my brother-in-law, "They must just think I make this shit up."

He said, "I don't think he did it on purpose."

And he was right, of course. I was sure my father felt terrible. I stayed outside in the dark and the cold and watched him bring the fan outside. I walked around the outside of the townhouses, trying to figure out what to do. I felt so unsafe. So lost. So damaged. My father came out and said he was sorry. I said, "I know but I have to stay out here for a while." I sat in the car, which had a VOC and hepa filter. I called Mario and told him I didn't know what to do. Finally I went back into the house. My father put his arms around me and apologized. I told him I knew he was sorry, but I couldn't stay there. I was still so upset. And I didn't feel safe. I knew that he felt bad. I felt like I should do something to make it better for him, but I didn't feel safe. I told him I had to leave until the spray dissipated.

I drove around Scottsdale in the dark. I didn't know where the hell I was. I felt desolate. Homeless. Victimized. Lost. Hurt.

Sick. My head throbbed. I felt like my lips were swelling. I called Mario in a panic. He tried to reassure me, told me I was probably just scared. I asked him to call my father and tell him not to worry or wait up for me; I'd be back in a couple of hours. I drove around wondering if there was any uncontaminated place in the world. Was there anyplace where I was safe, accepted, taken care of, loved, welcomed? Was there any place where I was not adrift?

No. And why should you be any different?

I went into some kind of weird Barnes and Noble or Borders called Bookstar. No one was there except the employees, and they were all laughing and talking about their sex lives. Or something. I didn't find any books that looked even vaguely interesting.

I felt like Homer Simpson at the beginning of the Simpson movie flipping through the Bible and then yelling, "There are no answers here!" There were no answers in that book store. Or in the next book store I went to.

I drove back to the townhouse. My father was asleep with the television on. My sister and bro-in-law were upstairs asleep. It was freezing in the house. My father had opened the windows to air it out. I woke up my father and told him to go to bed. He looked so cold and vulnerable. I got on the couch and pulled some blankets up around me. I didn't want to be there. I didn't feel safe. But I didn't want my father to feel bad. He didn't go to bed. We watched *Corner Gas* together and then *Becker*. Then he went upstairs to bed.

I tried to sleep. I think I got about three hours of sleep, off and on. I finally just got up at 4:30 a.m.—after I dreamed my sisters were all doing something that irritated me. I don't know what. I yelled at them. I said, "You're all fucking assholes!" And then I looked at my father and said, "Except you." Thinking of that dream made me smile. (When I told my sister and father the dream later, my dad said, "Gee, thanks, I guess.)

I got up and drove around Scottsdale in the dark again. It was about 5:30 a.m. Found a Starbucks. Sat inside sipping hot water. Felt alone, alone, alone. Lost.

Fuck.

And imagine how my father felt all the time now.

Later. . . .

I went to McDonald's with my father and sister and sat with them while they ate. Then went to Sears and Ace Hardware with my father. I gave him the keys to my car (his old car) and he drove for the first time in three weeks. My sister and I went to Goodwill to get me some clothes while Dad fixed the water heater.

When we came back to the townhouse, my father left to go to Ikea with another bro-in-law. He asked me if it was okay if he went. Of course it was all right. Live your life. Do what feels good. But I did feel bad. I'd come all this way and now he was leaving.

As he hugged me goodbye, he said, "I promise I'll throw out all those sprays."

I wondered if this was going to be the last thing between us. Would I never see him again and this is what we would remember? What *I* would remember?

It was all too hard and sad.

I sat outside the townhouse by myself and wondered what the fuck I was doing there.

I wondered what it would be like to be in a place or with a group of people who were always glad to see me, who welcomed me home, whose faces lit up when they saw me. Like Mario when he sees me. Wouldn't it be nice if there was more than one person in the world who really liked me? Who really valued me?

My sister and I took a walk before I left. We talked about what a good man my father is. How he just lives his life. How he faces life. Goes through it.

Then I was on the road again. Three hour drive back to Tucson because of traffic. Mario had spring rolls awaiting me when I got home. I wonder if he will ever know how much I love and appreciate him. I would be bereft without him.

That night, last night, I dreamed I went to a healer. She had all these little gadgets for me to help heal me. I told her I had once thought I would be a healer, but it didn't work out. I had too many doubts.

It was a long dream. I think it may have been the end of the world.

Or the beginning.

Ahhhh, I've talked too long. I can hardly keep my eyes open.

This afternoon as a big old coyote hid from my view and watched me, I walked to the Quail House. Once inside, I started a new novel, *The Blue Tail*.

We'll see what happens.

I had more to say. Or less to say. I'm not sure which.

May the coyotes sing for you. May the owls hoot for you. And I, I will root for you.

Always.

Blessed sea.

Year Five

The Fish Wife

A FOOL'S PROGRESS

December 14, 2008

We are here at the Old Mermaid Sanctuary! Yay! The coyotes are howling. The moon is spilling milky light all across the Sanctuary. Mmmmm.

We left LA county early this morning. We had frost on the car, and snow dusted the tops of the nearby mountains. We drove and drove, away from the cities and into the desert. We listened to the radio. Satish Kumar was on NPR. It was an interesting interview, primarily because the interviewer just didn't seem to understand Kumar and he sounded frustrated. "What do you mean you're never stressed? What do you mean you never hurry? How is that possible?" And Kumar said he did everything slowly. "Don't you feel the burden of trying to change the world?" Kumar said he wasn't trying to change the world—and yes, indeed that would be a burden. "I serve the world," he said. "I don't try to change it."

Wow. And wow. And more wows! I felt one of those quantum shifts people are always talking about.

To be in service to the world rather than trying to change it. All at once I understood when people said they were in service to God. It didn't have to be a groveling on their knees kind of service. It's what I feel about the Earth, about the world. I do want to be in service to the Earth! Trying to change the world suddenly felt like incredible hubris; me saying I wanted to change the world was like someone else saying they wanted to change God, I supposed.

To serve the world. To serve the world.

Later a big ole truck roared past me, too close, too loud. For a moment, I wanted to scream at him, give him some appropriate sign language. But then I thought, "Does that serve the world?" And I knew it didn't. My annoyance disappeared and I continued on my journey.

We arrived at my dad's place in Scottsdale around 3:30 p.m. I got to see two of my sisters, one of my bros-in-law, and my mother's psycho cat. (The psycho cat is another story.) It was good to be with everyone. Mario and I gave my dad one of our old laptops. Dad was a happy camper. It felt nice to be of service to my poppy.

Now we're in Tucson, or just outside, on the foothills of the foothills of the Rincons. We brought in all of our stuff from the car, and then we went out into the moonlight. We said hello to the horses, then hello to the Quail House, the place where I wrote *Church of the Old Mermaids*. Something ran in front of us in the moonlight. Desert faeries? A mountain lion? Coyote? Only fools walk in the desert at night.

Time for dreams. We're listening to KXCI, Tucson's community radio. I'm so tired I think I've fallen into a kind of trance. I know the DJ is speaking English, but I can't understand a word he's saying.

Outside somewhere it is snowing. Somewhere else it is raining. And the mountains are dreaming. Shhh. If you listen too hard, you will never hear them. If you don't try to listen, you will never hear them.

Something is happening here. And there.

BARRIERS

December 17, 2008
I am in my beloved Sonoran Desert at the Old Mermaids Sanctuary. At least that's what I call it: the Old Mermaids Sanctuary. It is the place where the Old Mermaids walked up out of the wash and began telling me their tales.

Things are different here this time. They are always different. And they are always the same. My arm hurts for one. It's really from my back. And I am sure it will dissipate, once I relax, once I acclimate, once I get accustomed to this place. In the meantime it makes life interesting, to say the least. And I still don't know what I'll write or where I'll write it or if I'll write. Maybe I will sit near the palm tree and just listen to the sound the dry leaves make when the desert wind shakes them.

The owls are nowhere in sight. This will be the first year we have been here without an owl or two. We are hoping they return sometime this month. We have had the company of a hummingbird for the last couple of days. We've also seen a couple of rabbits, and a coyote watched us watching her/him.

The biggest change is one that is pretty difficult to fathom. It changes the whole way this part of the desert feels.

Those of you who have followed my adventures over the years know that when I come here, I wander the wash, just like Myla wandered the wash in *Church of the Old Mermaids*. I pick up stories in the wash. The wash runs through several properties and the people and other fauna in the neighborhood have always used this wash freely as a thoroughfare.

Until now.

We walked a little ways down the wash and were confronted by a "NO TRESPASSING" sign with two strands of barbed wire across the wash. Fortunately our housemates had warned us; otherwise I think I would have dropped down into the sand and sobbed. Or screamed bloody murder.

This part of the desert feels different now, no longer free, no longer safe. (Safe is a relative term, of course. The desert is never "safe," but it felt like the wash was safe from human danger.) Mario and I are still walking the wash, but I put the *fath fith* on us and hope we will be safe.

I was going to take a photograph of the new fence and sign, but I couldn't raise up the camera to do it. That would make it too real. It is too sad. Maybe later. Instead I took a photograph of our beautiful eating area in our casita. It reminds me of how this problem might be solved: Newcomers to the desert near the Old Mermaids Sanctuary put up a fence. Everyone in the area is very upset. So Sister Ruby Rosarita Mermaid invites the whole neighborhood over, they make soup together, and they let the fence-builders talk about how they feel about the way the world is going. They welcome the fence-builders and let them know they are all in this together. The newcomers feel as though they are a part of something, and the fence comes down.

It could happen.

More later.

REGRETTING ENDINGS

December 20, 2008

It has been a full day. And a sad one. My dad's brother, my uncle, died last night. He went into the hospital and didn't come out, so it brings up memories of my mother's death. And it's just sad. My father has lost three family members in the space of a year: my mom and two of his brothers. My friend Evine's husband just sat down and died unexpectedly several years ago. Years later, her brother and sister died unexpectedly the same week. I asked her how she dealt with it all. She said, "You grieve. You don't try to repress it. You grieve. And then you go on."

Not easy. Just necessary. Tonight we had dinner with a woman whose nephew was struck and killed by a train last week. He was 23 years old. How does a family deal with that? I don't know.

I came home and learned my uncle had died. I thought of all the time I had spent with him when I was a child. I used to go on camping trips with him, my aunt, and my cousin who was my age. My uncle had a temper and he would get very angry when he was driving. My aunt sat very close to him, like they were still sweethearts—which I think they always were. And my uncle would swerve the car (with the camper attached) and curse out errant drivers. I did my best not to annoy him.

Once my cousins and I were playing darts in his garage and

one of my throws was a little off and the dart hit the windshield of his car. Everyone else ran away. I stared at the dot on my uncle's windshield. Everyone knew that we were not to touch any part of his car. I thought about not telling him, but I knew he'd see the dot and someone would catch hell. So I waited outside for him to come home from work so I could tell him. He hated work. We all knew his job was not something he liked. (He got much more mellow once he retired.) I waited outside of the garage and paced and bit my fingernails and waited for him. I knew he would scream and yell and I would be in big trouble.

He drove up and got out of his truck carrying his black lunch box. He was wearing his work clothes. They were blue or khaki green. I can't remember which. I cleared my throat and told him what had happened. He didn't say anything. He opened the door to the garage and went inside. I followed him. He looked at the dot on the windshield, ran his fingers over it.

I can't remember what he said. Something like, "It's not so bad." Or maybe it was, "All right then." I don't know. I only remember he softened when I told him. He wasn't angry. I believed back then that he admired me for telling him. I don't know if that was true. But I know that I felt more relaxed around him after that.

He told me once that he and my aunt used to ride around on a motorcycle together, dressed in leather, and I loved that image of them. It's hard to imagine them apart.

Endings are so difficult.

I watched a DVD tonight of Bill Moyers interviewing Maya Lin. One of the things they talked about was the Vietnam War Memorial. She said that we are a young country, and Americans pretend that death doesn't exist. In other countries, they mourn the dead. There is ceremony and ritual. People wail and mourn. I thought that was an interesting observation. I certainly don't know how to mourn. It took me twenty years to get over the death of my dog and pony. I couldn't look at a photo of Linda or my mother for a year after they died.

There are some times when I wish I had never left my Michigan home, and this is one of those times. I miss that I am no longer a part of the lives of my relatives. They were the people I spent most of my life with until I was eighteen. And then I went away.

Regret is a nasty thing. I just looked the word up. It comes from the Old French "regreter" which means to "bewail the dead."

Perhaps our regrets are too silent. Maybe we should wail and rend our garments.

I don't know.

DREAMY DESERT LIFE

December 22, 2008
It's evening here at the Old Mermaid Sanctuary. Mario is making us vegetables which we will combine with Amy's frozen dinners which we will microwave. I'll take some Vitamin B to make up for the Vitamin B the microwave kills. We don't have a microwave at home, so we only use one when we're on the road, usually to heat water or to cook the occasional frozen dinner.

More than you wanted to know about that, eh? Read on. It only gets better. Or worse, depending.

We've been here a week now. It usually takes me about a week to acclimate. Before that time, I'll usually have a backache, a rash, depression, cravings for sweets. And I dream. I have had more dreams here in a week than I've probably had in a year. I did ask my psyche and the Universe for big dreams, to help me decide what to do while I was here.

One day I got a book from the library on plants and shamanism. I opened it at random and read something about having to abstain from sex and eat a particular diet in order to be able to talk to the plants. I said to Mario, "What horseshit. I don't need to stop having sex or eat a certain way for the plants to talk to me. If the plants want to talk to me, they will."

That night I dreamed of ayahuasca, a sacred (and psychedelic) potion made from plants that shamans and others use for healing and revelation. In the dream, Mario and I walked down a long stairway. At the bottom of the staircase was this huge bin of bright green goop which in the dream I knew was ayahuasca. (Even though in real life the drink is brownish.) People were standing and lying in the ayahuasca. I said, "No way. I'm not doing that. I am not the type of person who should do drugs." I figured the shaman was a fake. He said I didn't have to ingest it; I just needed to immerse part of my body into it. I didn't want to do that, but I did, and Mario disappeared.

In another dream, a Native American man was telling me about the plight of cayenne workers in another country. Days later I dreamed of cayenne again. This time I was melting a dark chocolate bar, putting chopped nuts in it, and adding a bit of cayenne to it. I kept making this again and again in my dream.

The plants were speaking to me after all, without me giving up sex or food.

Mario and I have been walking in the desert every day. We don't walk in the wash much because of the evil "no trespassing" sign. Instead we go to the park a mile or so away and walk amongst the saguaros and prickly pears and other desert flora. Today my father and my sister came out from Scottsdale, and we walked together. We saw a jackrabbit. Only the second one I've ever seen. They look mythological. Exaggerated. Lovely. Slender. With the longest loveliest biggest ears I've ever seen. Before my dad came, I asked all the wild things to come to the Sanctuary, so my father could see them and know that he still has connections in this world. We saw the jackrabbit, and storm clouds moved overhead.

On Solstice, Mario and I walked in the park. And I began a new novel. I won't say anything about it yet. I've been able to start novels lately, but I haven't been able to finish them. So we'll see what happens.

I had more to say but it's late at night and I am tired. I almost always get depressed when I come here, and it happened again. But I knew it would pass and it did, as soon as I began writing. When I write, it is one of the few times in my life when I feel a part of life, when I am not lonely. It's such a strange thing. Now I shall go to sleep and see what wonders await me.

TWO FAIRIES AT A DUSTER

January 9, 2009
It is warming up here. I can walk around without a jacket for part of the day. And we'll be leaving soon. *sigh* Still, I soak up the desert. Today I stood in the wash as two ravens (or crows) flew around me and down low over me, seemingly interested in something about me. When I went away, they went away. Interestingly enough, I had just written a scene where three ravens flew over my hera, Sara O'Brion. (Her surname has its roots in the name Bran which means "raven.") I loved listening to their wings in the dry desert air. It was just me and them, baby.

Mario saw a bobcat while we were here, did I say? Very cool. I still have not seen the bobcat this time. This has been the season of rabbits. Jackrabbits and cottontails. Everywhere. Even in my dreams.

Last night I dreamed one of the Obama girls needed my help, so I helped her.

Too many other dreams about death and dying.

Today we saw a small prickly pear cactus growing out of a saguaro limb, about ten feet off the ground. Funniest thing.

Wrote 6,500 words today. I still feel as though I'm in the hacienda where I left Sara. She is very pregnant. And it is summer in the Sonoran desert.

Tonight we went to the library book sale and bought way too many books—but they are great books. Books on folklore, mythology, Mexico.

Walking in the desert while I've been here, I have become more certain than ever that I know what I want. I have wanted the same thing for thirty years. But every time I articulate it, all I hear is, "but I can't because. . . ." Because I don't have any money. Because I'm afraid. Because I'm sick. Because I can't be around any remodeling. Because there is no place left where the water and air are clean. Blah, blah, blah. All these buts and becauses over the years.

I don't like to want things I can't get. This causes suffering. Maybe wanting anything causes suffering. And yet if you never want anything, how do you make plans for the future?

This is what I want and what I've always wanted: I want land and I want a place where people can come to seek sanctuary, to write, to do art, to learn about sustainability, to envision and create the world anew. Listen to this: One of my favorite books of all time is Doris Lessing's *The Good Terrorist*. You know what I remember about it, what I loved about it? This woman was part of a group of "radicals." They took over buildings which weren't being used in London and they lived in them. Squatted. And while the rest of the radicals thought of this as a political move, as a protest, the hera of the story (who is a wee bit amoral, I seem to recall) turns this squat into a livable house. She creates a home. I love the process she goes through to make it a home.

That is what I want. A piece of land to care for. A sustainable lovely place where people heal and recreate. What I want is my own Old Mermaids Sanctuary. In nearly every novel I write, my characters are constantly creating family and home.

Home, home, home. Mi casa, su casa.

Tonight after the book sale, we went to see a movie. The best part of the evening—besides being there with Mario—was that when we were at the ticket window, two teenage boys came dancing up to the line with wands, wings, and the general clothing of fairies. One of the boys was very blond. The other was very dark. They were beautiful, funny, and clever. No one talked to them. Except us. I told them they were beautiful, and we talked about sweet nothings. I hope they had a lovely time and that no one bothered them. Bothered them in a bad way, that is.

You just never know when fairies are going to show up in your life. So watch out for them.

FERTILE OLD MOON

January 11, 2009

It's full moon today. I'm looking forward to watching the moon rise up above the Rincons. We just got back from a long walk in the desert. Our shadows slow danced with all the other shadows. We saw signs of wildlife everywhere. Coyote prints. Bobcat. Rabbit. Birds. And I'm pretty sure a mountain lion print. I loved it all. I danced on the trail. Mario and I both completed the first draft of our novels today. He finished his this morning. I finished mine, *The Fish Wife,* about 3:30 this afternoon. Over the course of thirty hours I wrote 21,000 words. I am very happy.

I am happiest when I am writing. I feel absolutely like myself. I'm usually without fear. I am in terrible and wonderful places, but I know it will all work out one way or the other. This book was amazing. I say that about every book because every book is an amazing experience. When I finished it, I cried. It was hard to leave behind the world I'd been in.

Now we're going to get my manuscript printed so I can read it to Mario. And we'll eat dinner and have a treat, and watch a movie on the computer while we play a game.

I am so grateful.

Year Six

The Rift

PILGRIM

December 21, 2009
We left in the dark Sunday morning. Traveling away from the heart of the world for our annual pilgrimage to the Old Mermaids Sanctuary. I had sung to the weather spirits and whispered to the mountains and the dragon of the hills for days ahead of time. Now we said goodbye to the house and the land and drove away.

We stopped every hour to change drivers. At one rest stop, a group of scrub oaks grew up tall and lithe and looked like a grove of dryads caught in the dance. We bowed to them.

Later we went up and over the pass. I pressed my hands against the window in thanks. When the White Mountain came partially into view—she wore clouds like a veil—we stopped the car and made offerings to her and the weather spirits. The wind whipped the offerings away. And it was done.

We passed the dragon made visible and knew we were on our way. We waved.

We kept driving. The light on the distant hills was mesmerizing. Unlike anything we had seen on this journey in other years. Sweet light shafted the hills here and there, like giant spotlights, making the hills look like mountains, green and gold, never dull, never gray.

When it wasn't raining, hawks perched on fence posts in the

fields just beyond the highway. The hawks looked toward the road, waiting for some passing car to kill some passing creature. I loved the plump hawks but was glad not to participate in their feeding this day.

We saw crows everywhere on our journey: individual crows picking at dead things on the pavement and flocks of crows rising up from the trees and fields. There they were, our ever present road companions, at every rest stop. In every field.

Redding was nondescript. In our hotel room, I got emails from my father. He seemed to be recovering. Wished I could do more.

I slept some.

Monday

We began the morning driving through thick fog. Sometimes my vision was so impaired by the fog that I kept driving only on faith. It felt like one of those nightmares where I am driving with my eyes closed—or through a thick fog.

It seemed appropriate for this pilgrimage to the Old Mermaids Sanctuary, somehow, to have to make it through the fog. To come out the other side.

All my trips to the Old Mermaids Sanctuary are pilgrimages. I go to write. To rest. To be still. To walk with the wild things. To be in the desert is to be present to all things, to the possibility of death. The possibility of life. The fog only reminded me that the veil was thin between here and there.

The fog ended. I heard from my youngest sister. She said our pops looked good. I was glad to have some of us there looking out for our dad. On Saturday last, five of my friends and I had done healing work for my father. It felt powerful and loving. Before I left home Sunday morning, my dad emailed that he'd had the best night yet and asked me to thank the healers.

Sometimes life works in mysterious ways.

Near the end of the day, we drove The Grapevine, up and over the Tejon Pass and then down toward Los Angeles. I could feel the dragon in the land. Moving, stretching, twisting.

We found a place to stay the night. After dark, we went out to the spa by the pool near our room. We took off our shoes and socks, sat on the stone, and put our feet in the hot water—becoming mer creatures for the evening. At least part of us. The sound of the traffic seemed to surround us, as though we were at the bottom of a circular waterfall, only it wasn't soothing like a waterfall. It felt intrusive and overwhelming. I got up and turned on the jets of the spa. The sound of the traffic disappeared.

We kicked the water. I closed my eyes. I whispered, "Hello." And then I felt as though the disappeared and displaced creatures from all around came to be near us. "I had nothing to do with this," I said. "I wouldn't have paved paradise." Although I wondered if it was true that I had nothing to do with it: After all, I was sleeping in a place where they had paved paradise. "What can I do to make up for it?"

Sing.

I looked around. Was that a rowan tree heavy with berries near us or some other tree disguising itself as the rowan on this Winter Solstice night? Weren't rowan trees notorious fairy hangouts? There was something wholly natural about this tree in such an unnatural setting. The red berries hung down from the branches like tiny edible rubies waiting to be plucked.

I could feel the real place beyond the concrete, beyond the traffic, underneath. Underneath.

Under the Earth I go....

I opened my mouth and sang. A wordless song. A song of recognition. Everything got still as I sang.

All that has passed away, all creatures, the flora, the shape of the earth, all these beings are mi familia.

It seemed as though the world settled into place as I sang.

Or else I did.

Eventually we shook the glittering scales off our feet and legs and got out of the water. Nothing looked the same any more, or any different. Mario and I held hands and went back to our room.

Tuesday

In the morning, we drove away from the dragon place and headed east to the desert. Blue-black clouds hung from the sky like a heavy theater curtain ready to drop. Eventually the clouds moved north and the sun came out. At a rest stop a hummingbird greeted us. Our first desert creature. The dirt beneath our feet was pink and diamond-colored.

On the radio news, we heard the wind had kicked up a dust storm on I-10, not far from us. The dust had became a cloud and moved over the road. People died in collisions and explosions. I stood on the pink dirt and called out to the wind. *Be calm, be calm.* The wind snapped the flags at the rest stop. I didn't remember ever seeing sustained wind like this in Arizona before.

We drove deeper into the desert. The low mountains hunkered into the ground. Saguaros raised their arms in greeting. I recognized this land. I knew it in my bones.

After a while, ahead of us, a strange kind of fog moved, only we knew it wasn't fog. We talked about what we would do if visibility got bad. We realized we had no idea what was a prudent course of action in a dust storm. I wondered if this was what the West would become as the climate changed and the top soil continued to erode: a giant dust bowl à la Oklahoma? We should all be prepared for this.

I thought of the dream I had last week about tornadoes. I could see small one and huge ones all across the landscape. In fact, I couldn't see the land, only the storms. In the dream, Mario and I tried to get to my father. We passed through the wall of the tornado unharmed. Later we survived a tsunami. We ended up at an old farmhouse, or some such—some kind of amazing house made from dirt, sunlight, and darkness.

As we watched the dust storm now, I sang for rain. Wouldn't rain stop a dust storm?

We kept traveling through the dust. Visibility never got bad or dangerous. Yet it felt apocalyptic. As though everything had changed and we just didn't understand that yet. We were all living a life that had already passed us by.

Then it began to rain. Arizona monsoon rain. Only this was December. The sky was black. The dust storm disappeared into the ditches to be resurrected another day.

The rain followed us to the Old Mermaids Sanctuary. It stopped while we unloaded the car. Then it rat-tat-tatted the roof while I put away our things in our casita. It rained as I thought about how grateful I was to the people who owned this place, who built this place, who loved this place, who are this place. I thought about how this place had saved my life. How I would not be the person I am today if it wasn't for this place where I go and listen to the voices of the desert. Where I listen for the heartbeat of the world. Where I sing with the coyotes.

When the place felt like ours again, I went outside and stood at the edge of the rain. And I sang. The rain came down harder as I sang. Water splashed up all around me. It was so dark out I felt a little spooked. I thanked the weather spirits for helping us get here safely. I heard thunder. I shivered and went back inside. I could almost hear the desert calling out to me, "You can run, but you can't hide!"

It is true: In the desert you can't hide anything. It's all out in the open. One way or another, if you stay long enough, the desert will show you the truth. Every year here I learn things about myself and the world I didn't know before. Sometimes they are things I would rather not know.

But I am not going to think about any of that tonight. I am not going to think about my father's surgery in a few days. Or about what novel I'll write while I am here. Not yet. Tonight I am going to fall asleep next to my sweetheart and listen to it rain in the desert.

Right now it sounds like the Old Sea is coming back to the New Desert. Perfect conditions for this pilgrim.

BY THE LIGHT

December 26, 2009

It is sundown in the Sonoran Desert. The edge of the east horizon is scarlet. A dog is barking somewhere. No sign of the great old horned owl that usually sleeps in the palm tree near the peanut-shaped pool. The east horizon, above the Rincon Mountains, is a delicate blue, almost turquoise, and I want to wear it, like a dress, with a scarf around my neck the color of the east horizon.

Mario has gone to town to get dinner. I have a headache. The sound of the heater is annoying. The light from the compact fluorescent bulbs hurts my eyes. I am certain one day they will tell us that exchanging all of our incandescent bulbs for these fluorescent bulbs was a bad idea. The light is stark and clinical. Incandescent light is . . . well, incandescent. Fluorescent bulbs aren't going to save us.

But I digress.

I am trying to unwind after a very scary and traumatic week. I woke up today feeling as though I'd been hit by a truck. As I stumbled out of bed, I could only imagine what my father felt like. (He had just had emergency heart surgery.) All day we kept getting good news about him. He was out of bed. He was joking around. They took out all his lines.

I felt more and less stressed all day. Mario started his new novel. I wondered if I would be able to begin my writing project. It is the reason we come here every year: to write in a beautiful (and sunny) place. But I need to relax. I did some meditation today, something I should do every day and do most days when I'm feeling good. It's those times when I don't feel like doing it that it would most likely benefit me.

This afternoon I have been thinking about why I write about taboo subjects. I have been writing on a blog for a long time now, since 2003. I've written about politics, my fury and despair over the Bush years, my depression and anxiety, food, nature, my travels, my writing, ecstasy, and various other things. I've had people I know say, "Do you really want to say these things in public? It's so personal."

It's an interesting question with a simple and complex answer. I have been writing since I was five years old. Writing was always how I communicated with the world. It has also been how I figured out the world and myself. I have written publicly about my own struggles with depression and anxieties because I think it's important to do so. Depression is still one of those things that people do not talk about. And anxieties or fears are even more taboo subjects. In fact, any kind of illness, especially so-called "mental" illnesses, are restricted topics of conversation. There is still so much shame attached to any kind of mental illness.

But mental illness is not a character flaw. Having fears and anxieties is not a character flaw. No one wants to be mentally ill. No one can just "snap out of it." No one gets depressed or becomes fearful on purpose.

For years I didn't tell anyone about my off again on again depression—besides numerous therapists. And no one knew about any of my fears. Even today when people who have known me for years find out, they often say, "But you seem so confident. I can't imagine you afraid of anything."

I think the people who have fears and who carry on with their lives are the bravest people in the world. If you aren't afraid of anything, you aren't brave; you're just clueless and/or lucky as hell.

So I write about depression. I know how lonely and hopeless it feels. I know we are so brave for trying to struggle our way out of this damn proverbial paper bag. I want everyone who has depression or who has had depression to know that they are not failures, they are not unlucky, and there is light at the top of that paper bag.

And it helps me to write about it. I still don't talk about it much. People don't know what to say when I do speak of it. I told a friend about it once and she said, "I don't have time to be depressed." At my two year Celtic Visionary and Healing Arts program, I told one of the participants about feeling depressed and she said, "It's because you aren't connected to the Divine Source." Neither of these responses was appropriate or compassionate. What they should have said is something along the lines of, "I'm so sorry. I'm here to listen if you need a sympathetic ear."

Another strange thing I write about publicly is my relationship with the Invisibles. I write about faeries and plant spirits and other such goodies. And I talk to faeries and plant spirits and other such goodies. I come to all this honestly. I grew up in the country, and my best pals were the trees and plants and animals all around me. I didn't get people. What they said often contradicted what I believed the truth to be. (You know what I mean. For instance when parents say, "Nothing's wrong. Every thing's okay," when actually everything is wrong and nothing is okay.)

But trees! Ahh, they were my saviors. I'd climb The Lullaby Tree, sit on one of her limbs, and sing for hours. It was my favorite place in the world, that place where the woods met the marsh. I left food for the hawks in an old scraggly evergreen. I named rocks and had conversations with them. I stood at the edge of the marsh and watched for *ignis fatuus* and flying saucers. And I had an entire "imaginary" world where the girls and women had magical powers (and men and boys didn't). I was only visiting Earth and disguising myself as an Earth girl to learn about Earth ways.

As a child, I spent most of my time out of doors. It was my father who taught me the names of the flora and fauna. It was my father who sniffed the air and said it smelled like snow and from then on I knew what the air smelled like just before it snowed.

I was completely in love and entranced by the natural world. It is no wonder or surprise that as an adult I would rekindle my love affair. I have experiences with plants that are just as real as my experiences with human beings. So why would I doubt the veracity of them? And of course, I write about them.

I believe we have more than six senses in our beautiful bodies. If we're open to the possibilities, who knows what we can sense, what we can experience? When I was a teenager, I wanted to be a scientist. I still consider myself a scientist: I am constantly studying and learning about this old world of ours. There is so much more to learn.

I suppose I could say I write about what I know, but I also write about what I don't know. Sometimes in the writing of it, I learn more or realize I know less. I write about what I love, but I also write about what I despise. Sometimes in the writing of it, I change my mind. I write about my life because it is fascinating to me. Sometimes I am amazed I get through the bad stuff; sometimes I am amazed at the charmed life I lead. But in the end, it's what I do. I write. I live. I write some more.

Ain't I lucky?

Mario just got home from the grocery store. He brought me a present: incandescent light bulbs. We go around the room and put them in here and there. The room feels better immediately, more homey. Softer. I'm sure all the Invisibles in this room quite agree with me.

Or maybe it's just me. But I feel positively glowing.

SHIMMER

January 6, 2010

It is dusk and I'm sitting in the Quail House working for the first time since I arrived here at our retreat. This is the first time I've felt relaxed since we got here. Well, maybe not the first time. When I was doing healing work for my dad. I was relaxed. I was in the flow. Felt like I was doing something. And no story was knocking on my subconscious demanding to be written. No character was whispering in my ear.

It's not that no stories are coming to me. Stories always come to me. One on top of another. Sometimes I think that's why I worry so much. My mind, or my imagination, jumps from the fact of what is happening this moment to what could happen. And usually it's not a happy ending. I do that when I see a movie, too, and when I read books. It's not a lot of fun. Because in the movies and books, I'm usually right—I guess the middle and the ending. Thank goodness in real life I am often wrong.

But who cares about that right now? Right this second the sun has plunged into the Pacific Ocean hundreds of miles away and the splash is painting our desert sky first lavender and now rose. Now it's adding gold to the structures near and far. The tree trunks which hold up the roof of the Quail House are black tinged with gold. In this light, they look edible. Dark chocolate.

Everything shimmers.

And the desert is so quiet I could hear a feather drop.

I had an epiphany about my father yesterday. I couldn't make it all better. If something happened to him, I would be devastated, but it wouldn't be my fault.

I have always thought it was my job to fix the world and everyone in it. Yes, people have told me that takes a lot of hubris. Maybe. But it didn't feel that way when I was a child. It just felt like that was my job. Especially since I was so empathic. When I was about twelve I saw the *Star Trek* episode "Empath." As I watched it, I was horrified and excited. I whispered, "That's what I am." (Horrified because she had to sacrifice herself in order to heal others.)

Oh my.

The inside of this tiny studio is now golden. The sky is pale blue except in the places where pink clouds stretch across it like the aurora borealis. The cactuses crowding the windows all seem to be reaching up, up, trying to tickle the belly of the sky.

I don't believe in suffering for the sake of suffering. I have never seen any benefit to being empathic. In fact, it often felt pathetic. I always wanted to be tough. Tough but loving. Fierce compassion. Fierce love. The other day my husband told me he saw me as tough.

"Really?" I said. "But I have so many fears."

"You get knocked down and you get back up," he said. "You keep going through it all."

That was not how I viewed myself at all. I often chastised myself for not overcoming my fears.

"So what: you see me as a kind of Clint Eastwood character?" I asked.

"Yeah, kind of," he said.

I laughed and thought, "But he's a Republican, isn't he?"

I didn't want to be sensitive. I didn't want to be empathic. So many people seemed to go through life successfully without ever having a clue to the suffering all around them. Or to the beauty all around them.

Ah. It is almost dark. A raven just flew by. Where the sun was is now a spray of scarlet. No, darker red. Bloody red. I feel that shiver that comes at twilight. Do I go out now while it's light to make my way back to the house? Or do I stay here a while longer, until it's dark, and then make my way through the possible javelinas, cougars, and coyotes?

Doctors used to tell me that I was like a canary in a mine. People like me got sick or were sensitive to things others weren't, but that didn't mean others weren't in danger. I never liked that analogy. I kept imagining those poor bright yellow canaries dropping dead and then the miners running for their lives to outrun toxic fumes. What good did that job do the canaries? I did not aspire to be a canary.

Now I know that being sensitive and empathic is not a weakness. I just notice more *things* in my environment than other people do. That can be a pain in the ass for me. I used to hate it. Now I realize it is a part of who I am.

I started this post to write about something else. Instead the shimmer of dusk brought me to this. To this question of identity. I thought people went through identity crises when they were teens. Or young adults. I have seen myself as a writer almost my entire life. Since I was five years old at least. I was defined by that part of who I was. A friend of mine once told me he was afraid of what would happen to me if I couldn't write.

When I first got sick, I couldn't write for over a year. I let go of the idea of being a writer. I went to school for another career. But then the stories returned, and I was able to delve into my imagination without my brain twisting in the wind of anxiety.

Now I know I am still a writer, but there are other ways I can be in the world. In my stories, a lone woman is always finding community. That's my theme. That's my search. A search for home. More and more I am finding home in nature again. In places where words aren't needed.

Maybe we invented words to try to celebrate Nature. It was a kind of art, this invention of words. To recreate the beauty all around us. To praise it. So we formed words to emulate life, the way a painter forms colors on her palette.

And now sometimes words get in our way. They're used to obfuscate rather than clarify. They're used to bore rather than enchant. They're used to lie, rather than truth tell.

Today my friend Joanna gave me the word "shimmer."

It sent a shiver up my spine.

It is an enchanted word.

It opened a door and a story walked through it. Or rather a group of characters did. Now they're sitting all around me, waiting for me to listen. I will try to invent sentences to recreate what they tell me. Invent sentences to praise what they say.

It is completely dark outside now. Inside this House of Quail, the golden tail of the tiny ceramic mermaid on the window sill glitters in the dim light. I know it is time to step into the darkness and see what is out there.

Year Seven

The Desert Siren

SINK OR SWIM

January 14, 2011

I'm sitting in the Quail House looking out at a forest of cholla trees. One lone scraggly creosote branch grows up among them all. Above, and nearly all around, is blue, blue sky.

Linda Ronstadt and Ann Savoy are singing "Adieu False Heart" on my computer and the hepa-VOC filter whirs behind me, muffling the sound of distant machinery that breaks the quiet on the Sanctuary today.

Before I began to write this morning, I stood outside to talk to the Desert and her creatures. I could almost feel the motion of the Old Sea beneath my feet and all around me. I nearly always hear a siren song in this desert—and often I feel at a loss as how to interpret it.

This year has been a tough one on the Sanctuary for me. I'm not sure why. Three winters ago, we only spent a couple weeks here, trying to recover from the sudden death of my mother. Last year, my father had major open heart surgery. Every day I came into this Quail House and sang a healing song for my father. I had a knot in my stomach the whole time. I started a novel, *The Rift*, but I never finished it here. This year, I thought it would be great because my family was safe and sound, knock wood.

But I have felt anxious the whole time, and I haven't felt physically well. I've been angry because I didn't feel well. I struggled with asthma every time I took a walk; I had a sinus infection and one cold sore after another. On top of it all, I had this sinking feeling that I was failing at everything.

Mostly I was exhausted from a year of changing my whole life again and again and again.

Maybe not my whole life, but a lot of it.

I changed too many things to go into now.

Let's just say it was a rocky year, and the first few weeks at the Sanctuary seemed to mirror this rocky road. I felt crappy and crappier.

And then last Saturday morning, Mario happened to look at CNN on his computer and he found out there had been a shooting at a Safeway in Tucson a few miles from here; Representative Gabrielle Giffords had been shot along with many others.

I started to cry. We don't have a TV here, or a radio that works, so I searched desperately for online news. I knew little about Gabrielle Giffords. The ranchers I interviewed for my jaguar book last year had said Giffords had tried to help them out with the problems they were having on the border. I didn't know if she was a Republican or Democrat at first. I didn't care. I was just horrified that once again someone had gone on a shooting spree.

I wasn't surprised it had happened. I had been holding my breath since the presidential election, in fear that someone was going to go after one of our elected officials.

I had seen it before. I was nine when President Kennedy was murdered. When it happened, I pinched myself to see if I was dreaming: I couldn't believe someone would kill the president.

And then Martin Luther King was murdered. And Bobby Kennedy.

I grew up as a witness to so much violence in our country. My formative years were the sixties, and the entire world—beyond our little house in the country—seemed tinged in bloody violence.

It also seems that any time a Democrat becomes president, the crazies come out of the woodwork, frothing at the mouth and bent on vengeance.

But vengeance for what? It is as though an entire segment of our country feels entitled to rule the world. Elections don't matter to them. They want their people in office no matter what. When it doesn't happen, they go crazy. Or maybe they take off their tin hats and crazy happens.

I am such a bleeding heart liberal that I am always disappointed with whomever is elected. They are never liberal enough for me. I can't understand why everyone doesn't want a safe and clean environment. I can't understand why it matters to anyone if someone else is gay. I can't understand why it matters to anyone whether someone who is pregnant decides to terminate her pregnancy or not.

So no one politician ever fits my particular bill exactly.

But just because they don't agree with me doesn't mean I have ever wanted any violence done to them.

Years ago, I loathed the government, and I wasn't shy about saying so. It seemed like every politician was bought and paid for by some corporation. It didn't seem like anyone was working for what I cared about.

Then the Oklahoma City bombing occurred. When they arrested Timothy McVeigh, they kept mentioning that he had anti-government sentiments. I remember standing in front of the television looking at the smoldering Alfred P. Murrah Federal Building and thinking, "I am not like him, I am NOT like him." I had criticisms of the government, but I was not like him.

And yet, I was making broad judgments about people. I wasn't working to change anything in my community at that particular time. I was just complaining.

I decided then and there that I would be careful with my words. I would no longer badmouth the government just to badmouth "it." The government was made up of we the people. We are the government.

During the Bush years, I was appalled by what he and his administration did. I was repulsed. I was furious. I felt that many of their policies were contrary to what our country stands for. But I never wished any of them ill. I wanted them out of government via elections. I worked hard in our peace group. I worked hard to get politicians elected who shared my values.

When Barack Obama became president, it seemed like even more crazies came out of the woodwork than they had when Clinton was elected. Only now they had a television network dedicated just to them. They had radio personalities urging them on. I had been afraid since day one that someone was going to get shot. The anti-immigrant rhetoric, especially in Arizona, was frightening. I had lived in Arizona twenty-five years ago, and the politics then were strange and bigoted. (The governor wouldn't even recognize Martin Luther King Day.) Now it seemed even more volatile.

This is a long way of saying that I wasn't surprised when I heard about the shooting in Safeway. I was appalled, grief-stricken, horrified, but I was not surprised.

I had seen too much of this over my lifetime.

I'm exhausted thinking about it. More and more I feel out of step with the world. I hear more and more people say they don't like people and they can't stand being around other people.

I keep thinking of this old science fiction story I read thirty plus years ago where no one ever left their homes. They stayed inside, isolated from everyone else. Is that what will happen to us?

I'm always wary when someone says they don't like people, when someone says they would much rather spend time with animals. I love domestic animals like I love people: one at a time. I am most comfortable in the wild, communing with the wild things, the plants, animals, the Invisibles. But I understand that human beings are my tribe. If I hate people, then I hate myself.

It seems so easy to say, "I love animals." It's like saying you love being around a nine-month-old child. A baby can't question or judge us, neither can animals.

Are we forgetting how to have relationships with other people? Are we forgetting how to be in community with others of our own kind?

Relationships with other human beings are difficult. But don't we have to figure it out? I mean, we can't live without each other. We're either going to sink together or learn to swim together.

After a lifetime of living around violence, I am nearly always on the lookout for it. It's understandable. In every group of women I've ever been with, nearly all of them have either been raped or sexually abused as children. Nearly all of them have been a victim of some kind of violence over the years. I am wary most of the time—and I think it's smart to be careful.

But there is a difference between being careful and hating other people.

A few days after the shooting at Safeway last Saturday, Mario and I went out to a movie here in Tucson. I had brought a stone with me, a little moss agate. I dropped it in the middle of the movie. After the movie was over and the lights came up, I began looking for this little stone. Immediately, three or four people started looking with me. These complete strangers were crouched down looking at the filthy floor, trying to find my little fifty cent stone.

I was so moved by this act of kindness and I felt such love for these strangers that I wanted to hug each and every one.

I restrained myself.

We never did find the stone. But I felt buoyed by the experience.

I don't know what I'm trying to say.

I'm sorry there's so much violence.

I'm sorry those people were killed.

I hope beyond hope that the crazies out there will settle down. Take a chill pill. Help someone find their lost rocks.

I am going to try to be better at forging relationships with people. It's difficult. I have to learn to go with someone else's flow. I'd rather hide sometimes. Or at least I'd rather write a book. That seems much easier.

So often when I'm around people, I feel a little seasick. But then, even when I'm not around people, I feel a little seasick. Maybe it's not them; maybe it's me.

In either case, I'm going to dive right in.

Maybe I should learn to swim first.

THE WILD KEEPER

February 3, 2011

What if we each pledged to care for a plot of land? It could be a square foot, the footprint of the place where we live, a piece of property we own, or a park we love. We would care for these pieces, these plots, these Earthly parcels, like we would care for our fingers or our arms or our legs: We would recognize that it is all a part of us, and as the land is cared for, so are we.

Sometimes I close my eyes and I can see all these pieces of land like pieces of a quilt. We could link them all up, put them all together, and then we would have one beautiful quilt of the world. It's already there, this quilt, so perhaps our jobs—as caretakers—is to repair the torn pieces, re-stitch those places where the thread has come out, and clear away the debris.

Because I'm a writer, I often see the world in metaphor—the land is like our body, the land is a quilt, the land is our mother. But I feel the world in my bones, too. I breathe the world in and out. I take off my shoes and I step on the grass, on the dirt, on the earth, and feel my soles against the soul of the world. I feel the Earth—Nature—beneath my feet like an ocean wave and I know I should grab a surf board and enjoy the wild ride.

Sometimes I feel the Wild pulsing in my own soul and I know it is Nature speaking to me, through me. I feel as though my creative force and my passion for the world is Nature working her art through me: I am her art piece.

I like finding others who are not like-minded but like-souled. Is that a word? I crave the wild. I don't do extreme sports. I'm not a good camper. I don't climb mountains. I have a need to be out of doors, but it's not to prove anything to myself or anyone else. It is like drinking water or eating food or breathing air. It is as necessary as all of those things. I feel myself shrinking and changing when I cannot be in a place where the wild things roam.

Years ago, I heard that jaguars were coming back into the American Southwest. Two of them had been photographed. My heartbeat quickened. I began to dream of jaguars. They were always powerful, frightening, and alluring. I felt as though this cat was speaking to me, as though these jaguars meant something to me, personally, as well as to the world. I wanted to write about them. I began talking to people about jaguars.

I wanted to find people who understood about the wild.

And so I found Sergio Avila, a biologist who was working for Sky Island Alliance. One year we talked about how to protect and conserve the jaguars in the United States. One year we talked about the death of one of the jaguars after it was captured and collared. Sergio and I spoke a common language about nature.

I found other people who lived on the land and understood the ways of the wild, too. I talked to ranchers and hunters and biologists and conservationists. Many of them were trying to save and protect their lands and their livelihoods. All of them wanted to make certain the land was viable for the wild creatures, in one way or another. They didn't all agree with one another. Some felt sad, angry, and betrayed by what happened after the collared jaguar died.

But that is another story for another day. I will piece together that story soon. Now I want to think about the living wild.

One day when Sergio and I talked about the wild world, he told me about Carlos Robles Elías, a rancher in Sonora, Mexico. He had 10,000 acres and he was dedicating it to wildlife conservation. A wild jaguar and several ocelots had been photographed on the ranch. You must speak with him, Sergio suggested; he could be the hero of the book you are writing. I felt the hair stand up on the back of my neck again, just as it had when I first learned about the jaguar.

And so one day, I was in a truck with Carlos and my husband, and we were driving down windy Sonoran roads. The truck shook from a bad tire, but we drove toward El Aribabi Conservation Ranch and we talked about conservation. I scribbled in my notebook while Carlos talked, and I looked up occasionally at the landscape around us. It looked familiar. Had I been here before?

Carlos spoke passionately about conservation. He wasn't certain how he had come to his views, but he thought it had a great deal to do with his older brother who would talk to him about nature. Carlos had moved the cattle off of his ranch. He wanted to make his ranch a paradise for wildlife and show his neighbors how it worked. They were waiting to see if he would be successful at it. Could it be economically feasible?

I told Carlos that in my country if someone owned 10,000 acres they were rich. He said he was not rich. He was struggling. He wanted to make enough money to have a normal life with his wife Martha and their three children. "I don't want a Hummer," he said. "Or anything like that. I want a normal life."

And on his piece of land, his parcel of Earth, he wanted to make a home for the wild. He wanted to make his conservation ranch viable so that "wildlife would have a home forever." He believed the most important thing was a massive education program, about trash, about conservation, about wildlife. Now people throw trash on the ground and don't even think about it, he said. When someone sees a snake, they think they have to kill it.

"If we educate the children about the snake," he said, "then they won't feel they have to kill it and they will keep it alive."

He has school children come out to the ranch and play in the stream. He wants them to know what it is like to be in nature.

I nodded and wrote as he talked. It always surprises me that people need to be taught about nature, that they don't feel an innate connection with the environment. It was, I supposed, like teaching people they had a heart. They couldn't see it, but it kept them alive.

As we drove, Carlos spoke about his ranch. He had over thirty protected, threatened, and endangered species on the land, including a jaguar and several ocelots. He had over 180 bird species. He told me the jaguar came up to his land to live because it was a quiet place, a protected place.

Carlos pointed out areas along the route where the land had been overgrazed. It wasn't just that too many cattle were bad for nature, he said; it was that the cowboys would kill anything. They saw something wild, and they'd shoot it, especially mountain lions.

Soon we arrived at the ranch. We went through the gate and passed by huge old cottonwood trees. They looked like old naked dancers, reaching up to the sky or off to the side to stretch. They looked like guardians, too, and I waved. I'd like to talk with them. What had they seen over the years?

Below the ranch house a stream wove its way through a copse of cottonwood trees. Or maybe it was the other way around. The cottonwood were drawn to the water. Something profound and glorious about water in the desert, always.

Carlos took us out onto the ranch. He drove slowly through a mesquite forest. Several of the mesquite trees were huge and hundreds of years old. Mesquite roots go very deep—they know how many secrets are buried in the dirt—and I wondered how far down the roots of these ancient trees went. Some of the trees were much younger and had several small trunks instead of one large one. They had come up after Carlos's grandfather bulldozed the area 40 years earlier and planted grass for the cattle.

We drove on the ridge tops, following the line of the hills, looking down at the grasslands. I thought for certain we would see a mountain lion in these blond grasses. I could feel them all around us. This place was more wild than any African savannah. More desolate. And beautiful.

Eventually we stopped on one of the ridges to wait for Sergio, who had just arrived at the ranch house. Below us were the hilly grasslands, dotted with yucca. Around us in all directions were the ancient mountains, slouching into the earth, their jaggedness rounded off from age or experience. On many of the nearby slopes, we could see wildlife tracks going through the tall grass. Carlos pointed to a peak just beyond: That was where they had photographed the jaguar.

We were in jaguar country.

I loved listening to Carlos talk. He knew every inch of these wild lands. And they were wild lands, make no mistake about that. It was a harsh landscape filled with wild life: rattlesnakes, mountain lions, bears, bobcats, foxes, ocelots, and a least one jaguar. This wasn't the prairie where you'd take a snooze on the soft grass. This wasn't a temperate forest fairy land. This was harsh dry country. It made the hairs on the back of my neck stand up. It made my soles sweat. It was so silent and majestic; I felt my soul settle into my body and relax.

Take a deep breath. This is the wild. This is where you are most at home.

And this man Carlos was protecting this wild place. He was restoring the land so that it was a good home—so that wild life and people could thrive. People need wild places. Children need to play in wild streams. Men and women need to hear wolves howl and coyotes yip. People need to be connected to the wild. The soul's true nature is unleashed when it hears, senses, sees, dances the song of the wild.

I'm sure of it.

I knew Carlos only a few hours and I knew this: He felt the beat of the land in his heart. In his soul. Later, Carlos would say of Sergio (or Sergio would say of Carlos) that they understood each other because their common language was nature.

That is my language, too.

Later Mario told me we had been on the windy road to the ranch before. That was why it had seemed familiar to me. Several years earlier, I had felt the need to go to Mexico, to go out into the countryside, into the desert. I knew something awaited me there. I thought it was a home, a parcel of land that was calling to me. I wasn't sure. We drove down the road for a long while. We stopped the car and I stood in the middle of the road and listened to the silence. I breathed deeply and wondered what had drawn me to this place. Now all these years later I was back; only this time, I had someone who opened the gate for me, who invited me in.

Invited me to this wild place.

When Sergio arrived, we continued on the road, this time going down into the canyon. We saw a huge buck running up one ridge. The buck stopped and watched us for a time and then continued on his journey and we continued on ours. We drove to the canyon floor and stopped by two buildings in progress, one made from adobe, the other from local rocks. Carlos planned on using four energy sources for these buildings once they were completed: solar, wind, hydropower, and pedal power.

We walked past the houses, through the tall grass, and into the empty stream bed. Small leaves crunched beneath our feet. This was a dry place. The boy scouts had been out last summer doing restoration work in the stream. They put large rocks at various places in the stream to slow the water that came cascading down the canyon during the rainy season. This would help prevent erosion and allow the water time to soak into the ground and raise the water table. As we stood in the peaceful stream bed, we could feel the difference in temperature even though the creek was empty now. It was noticeably cooler. Since the scouts had done this work, the level of the water in Carlos's well had risen.

Carlos wanted to show everyone that many of these kinds of changes could be made quite simply. The boy scouts had done this restoration work in one day. Actions = results.

We talked about many things. Sometimes Carlos spoke in Spanish and Sergio translated. I often understood the gist of what he was saying, and always I understood the passion. He wanted his ranch to be a working model for sustainability. He wanted scientific research done here. He wanted a conservation school to be built here.

But right now, it was difficult for him to make a living off the ranch. Something had to change. They needed to get some kind of income so they could keep the land wild, and so they could keep doing research and restoration work.

I understood this dilemma. How to live in this world and do the right work.

Why did keeping the wild wild always come down to economics? Why was so much of life like that? Some old European towns used to keep a portion of their towns and communities wild. No one owned this land. Everyone cared for this land. It was where the ancient trees grew and the wild animals lived. When the conquerors came, they always decimated these commons and cut down the ancestor trees in an effort to destroy what the community held most dear.

Who are the conquerors now? We are decimating our own

commons. Is it because we can't feel the wild beating in our own hearts?

The four of us drove back to the ranch and had lunch under the portico along with several researchers from a Sonoran university. As I sat at the table eating, I wondered how Carlos could keep this land wild. I imagined desert gardens all around the ranch house—permaculture gardens. I imagined tables and chairs under the portico and people visiting from all over and paying for the privilege of being there. I imagined trails leading from the house to other places in the ranch. If gardens and trails were created near the house, all kinds of workshops could happen here. Writers and artists would want to stay at the house or go further out to be alone.

Or people could come who wanted to research or explore. Archaeological teams did that all the time: They charged volunteers to work for them. Couldn't something like that happen at the ranch?

It seemed like this place could become a sanctuary for humans as well as other wild life. A place to connect with the outer wild life and one's own inner wild life.

Carlos was trying to keep the wild wild. Sergio was doing that, too.

That was what I tried to do, in my way. With my wild words?

Not long ago, Carlos told us, someone caught an ocelot on their land and brought it to him to put on his land. He said no. When he told us this story, I said, "That's because you don't want this to be a zoo. You want this ranch to be a kind of template so that others can do that same thing on their own land." He wasn't a zoo keeper. He was a *wild* keeper. He wanted to make his land wild and demonstrate how others could do the same.

Later, Mario and I wandered around the house and then went down to the stream while Carlos and Jose changed a bulging tire on the truck. I liked being on the land. I liked my soles against this earth. Mario and I watched the sunlight hit the tops of the cottonwoods as the sun began to set. It was so quiet here. I felt peace in this wild place.

Still later, Carlos drove us back to the border. We talked of many things on the drive. When he stopped to drop us off, I shook his hand and thanked him for a wonderful day. Then Mario and I got out of the truck and walked across the border to our car. We drove for an hour or so to Tucson and stopped into a restaurant for a late dinner. We ordered too much food. I ate too much. I missed the land already. I missed the easy wild day.

I had to remember that the wild was always in me. I didn't have a parcel of land to care for. I had me. I had my words. Maybe in some way, that helps the world. I hoped Carlos could keep his land wild, for his sake, but also for the sake of the world. We will always need wild places and wild keepers.

Year Eight

Whackadoodle Times
Pricked: A Jane Deere Novel

WALKING IN PRICKLY BEAUTY

December 31, 2011

Once again I am at the Old Mermaids Sanctuary. It is named something else by other people, but that's what we call it. It is here where I first learned about the Old Mermaids when they came up out of the wash and told me their stories.

We've been here for nearly two weeks. It's been blue skies most of the time, and yesterday, it finally got warm. We take long walks in the desert; we take short walks in the wash. In the evening, coyotes serenade us. (Okay, they're probably serenading each other, but you get the idea.)

At dusk, we often see javelinas. One night when I was taking out the trash (down the long dirt drive to the road) a javelina followed me. She was either looking for love in all the wrong places or she wanted my garbage.

You pick.

I've also seen two roadrunners, once at the Catholic church near here where Mario and I went to walk the labyrinth. The second time was when I was in the wash. The one at the church seemed a bit thin and too interested in us. The one in the wash took one look at me, raised her tail, and sauntered away.

I believe that was the healthier response.

And of course, the Sanctuary is filled with rabbits and birds and cacti and my beloved agave, and mesquite and paloverde trees.

In the mornings, Mario goes out and writes in the Quail House. When he's finished he returns to the casita. I make him breakfast. Then I go out to the Quail House and work. When I'm finished, he makes me lunch. Then we go for a walk.

It is an idyllic life in many ways, these weeks we're here.

The first day I wrote here, on Solstice, I wrote an Old Mermaids Healing Tale. The second day, I wrote 10,000 words on my novel *The Rift* to finish it. I had started it here the winter my father had heart surgery and I hadn't finished it, until now.

On Christmas, we drove to Scottsdale to be with two of my sisters and their significant others and my father and my aunt Alice. We had a good time, but I was wired the whole day and didn't relax, as is often the case when I see my family for the first time on a visit. Once when I went home to Michigan, I was curled up in a fetal position for two days. I have no idea why. The members of my family are good people. We each have our own difficulties, like most people, although we rarely talk about them with each other. There is a tacit agreement, as there is in many families, to keep it light when we're together.

I've never been a keeping-it-light kind of person. When I was younger, I always wanted to talk about things, get them out in the open, solve problems. But I've gotten over that. Spilling your guts at a family gathering never does anyone any good as far as I can tell. So mostly I just try to get along and still be myself when I'm with family. I want them all to be healthy and happy—and since I was a kid, I have often felt responsible for their health and happiness.

I'm not certain if I was born that way or if I was created that way. I remember when it started. It was in first or second grade and one of my teachers took me aside and told me that the other kids looked up to me. I was a natural leader, she said, and if I was nice to Billy (the kid who pooped his pants in class, who always stunk, and who lived with the other poor people in Saxony subdivision), everyone else would follow my lead.

I was a naturally shy kid, so I'm not sure if anyone was looking to me for anything, but I listened to my teacher and I was kind to Billy. In fact, I became the little kid who was always standing toe to toe with the bullies trying to protect other kids, most especially one of my little sisters who was always getting picked on.

And I was the one who noticed things were wrong long before anyone else did and I'd try to get help. Tried to get help for my pony who was sick (she died). Tried to get help for one of my sisters who was starving herself. Tried to save the killdeer on school property that the boys were always trying to kill.

I was always trying to fix or save something or someone.

In any case, Christmas was wonderful this year and it was difficult. On the way home, in the dark, I heard Judy Garland singing, "Have yourself a very merry Christmas," on the radio, and suddenly I was remembering being a kid singing, "Yesterday," while I was on a swing, wishing my life was easier and I was happier. I was about ten years old! As I sat in the car next to Mario, I looked back at my life and I couldn't find one memory where I was happy. I was always so sad. And that realization made me sad. My whole life was just one big pile of unhappiness. Every memory I had was rife with illness and sadness.

When we got back to Tucson and the Sanctuary, I couldn't sleep. My mind raced. I could not turn it off or down. I kept thinking about the day. I should have said this to so and so. I should have said that to so and so. I should have made a better effort. I should have tried to have a conversation with so and so.

Oh. My. Gawd.

I knew it was ridiculous, but I couldn't shut it off.

I got a few hours of sleep and woke up miserable. And I still had a stupid cough from the flu I'd had two weeks earlier. I felt sick and depressed.

I looked at the photos I'd taken Christmas day. As we were leaving Scottsdale, Mario and I had stopped at the Franciscan Renewal Center to walk the labyrinth there. Mario had taken some photos of me. In one I'm on a swing and I'm smiling.

It was the first photo I had seen of myself in probably twenty years where I thought I looked like myself. Where I looked as though I was full of myself—which has always been my goal. I looked at the photo and thought, "I don't look sad. I look happy. I must be happy." I thought about this year. It was a difficult year for me. I felt like I was slip-sliding backwards. I was sick or depressed or anxious the whole year.

At least that's what I thought.

I knew it had been a bad year for many people. Friends of mine had lost family members. So many other people had lost homes and jobs and life savings. We'd all witnessed the horror of the earthquake and tsunami in Japan.

I'd finished school but at the end of it, I couldn't find a job. Any jobs in my field were shit jobs. The pay was awful, the hours were awful, and most of jobs were in hovels. I refuse to work for the good of society by having a shit job in a shit building. So that sent me into paroxysms of guilt. I'd just spent a very stressful year going to school. I'd spent our money, plus I'd gotten a loan from one family member and another family member had gifted me with money so that I could go. What had I done? Mario said it would come to something. It would have some meaning and value in our lives eventually.

But I didn't want to end up in the poor house or in the streets, panhandling. (Granted, we don't have poor houses any more.) Ever since I had gotten ill and had to quit my regular day job, I had tried to figure out a way to make a living in this ol' world. I had to do SOMETHING to be of value.

It had been a tough year in other ways, too. But I don't want to list all the crappy things that happened. Let's just say the whole year seemed like I was just dragging one foot forward and then jumping two steps back.

But as school ended, I realized two things. One, I realized again (again, again) that I am a storyteller and that's what I'm good at and it's what I want to do. Two, maintaining and strengthening a connection with Nature—particularly with plants—was where it was at for me. (Not in a botanical way, per se, but in that "let's talk to the plants and get groovy" kind of way.)

Mario and I had launched Green Snake Publishing in the fall of 2010. We started out slow, but once I got out of school this summer, we went crazy full speed ahead.

I began to love writing and publishing again, and my writing life began to blossom, as it were.

And yet in other parts of my life, I was still struggling. I started a permaculture guild in my community, but there was trouble in paradise right away. At first people wanted to be involved, but then hardly anyone was involved. And then when the Occupy movement came to the gorge, some people in the guild got offended by any mention of it and wanted it gone, gone, gone from the permaculture guild.

I was thrilled by the Occupy movement. After years of activism, I was exhausted. I didn't feel as though I had ever accomplished much. Seeing a new generation—and all generations—stand up for themselves and the environment was invigorating. I went down to Occupy Portland a few times.

I was also shocked by the invective directed at the Occupy movement. Here we were trying to make our country more democratic, more fair, more equitable for everyone, yet so many people were just hateful towards us. Someone in my own family wrote to me, "Let them come down here and we'll put them six feet under." When I pointed out that he was threatening my life, he continued to rant about how "they" should leave and go to another country.

What?

I was appalled by the ignorance. Our country is based in revolution, and pointing out what is wrong has always been a part of who were are as a nation.

Paradigm shifts are never easy.

Where was I going with all of this?

Was it a terrible year?

Yes.

Was it a wonderful year?

Yes.

I'm in the desert now. It's been a tough couple of weeks. I apparently somatize absolutely every feeling I have. Since I've been here I've had a cough, my feet have hurt, my hip has hurt, my back has hurt, and I've had insomnia.

I really think it would be easier on everyone if I just felt my feelings, whatever they are.

I am in the desert.

I love the desert.

I used to loathe it.

I love where I live in the Pacific Northwest. When I walk the great old forests, I feel as though anything is possible. I feel dwarfed by the bigness, by the awesomeness of the woods or the ocean or the rivers. I am a child or a bug or a puff of air. Small and probably insignificant.

When I am in the Southwest, I feel loved and accepted. I walk amongst prickly plants here. They all have prickles. I rubbed mesquite leaves across my cheek yesterday. They were nearly as soft as mullein leaves. And right there by the leaves was a thorn.

Could have cut my cheek deep if I'd rubbed my face a little differently.

Everything is prickly here, with a soft center.

I can relate.

Just call me Briar Rose. Not because I fell asleep for a hundred years, but because I am covered in thorns.

When I lived in Tucson twenty-five years ago, I liked the desert, but it scared me. That was the proper attitude. I love the desert. I feel at home in the desert. I feel welcomed in the desert. But I don't romanticize it. I know I could be dead in minutes should I get bitten by a snake. I could be dead in hours if I got lost on a hot summer day. I have to be alert. You can't let your mind wander in the desert. It is a constant teaching about being in the present.

The desert is a place for old warriors. A place for edge dwellers and crazy people. A place for peace mongers. A place for old dogs and new tricks.

I feel loved in the desert. Did I say that? Accepted.

I am battered and beaten up. My broken nose makes me look like one of those punch-drunk fighters. The white hair marks me as a desert dweller.

I fit in here.

The desert is where people throw trash, dead bodies, and beer bottles.

The desert is where some of us go to learn the language of our souls again.

For this coming year, I want to learn how not to be buffeted so much by the storms of my life. I want to be more Zen, in touch with the Tao, a more "be in the now, baby" kind of person.

Really, I just want to be more myself. I can't believe myself was destined for such a life of sadness and illness. But whatever happens to me, I'd like to get my mind right.

What I've tried over the years hasn't worked.

Or maybe it has. I've gotten here. I'm sitting across from the man I love. I am surrounded by beauty. Prickly beauty.

My kind of beauty?

This next year, I hope to walk, dance, play, and write in beauty. I hope it's an easier year for everyone.

This next year, I'm not going to try to save the world. I'm not going to try to save anyone.

Perhaps I will save myself?

This next year, I don't want to just survive: I want to thrive.

I wish the same for you.

May it be so.

THORNY PALACE

January 28, 2012

Today is our last day on the Sanctuary. We're nearly all packed. Tomorrow we'll leave before the sun is up. Mario is inside the casita preparing dinner. I am in the Quail House where I have as company a huge spider. She clings to an old blanket in the chair behind me. Perhaps she is waiting to hear stories from me, or else she's come to share some of her own.

Outside the wind blows, stirring up dust and memories of winters past.

I lean my head out the top half of the Dutch door and listen. Does the wind bring me more stories? Coyote serenades? Bobcat purrs? Mesquite wisdom? The secrets of the paloverde?

I came here a month ago still recovering from the flu. For the first few weeks, I felt a bit battered. A rough year had taken its toll. I felt unmoored by dynamics in relationships I didn't understand. And when I felt I did understand, I didn't. Why was it that some people felt lifted up when they were trying to bring someone down? I have encountered this throughout my life. Because I often appeared confident, people saw this as an opening to try to degrade me—knock me down a few pegs.

Confidence was not a characteristic often valued, especially in women.

It often seemed that some of the people in my life—friends, family, acquaintances—liked me better when I was ill or not myself, when I was failing rather than succeeding.

Mario believes this is often true with many people, especially those who leave their familial environs. "The tribe doesn't want us to change," he says. "That's why people who go away are often teased or belittled when they return for a visit."

Often if we know something, we're accused of being know-it-alls. And if we're good at something, we're accused of not working hard enough or not deserving what we have.

I don't understand this attitude.

I like to be around people who are smarter than I am. I like it when people know more than I do. I like it when people I know and love are successful. I love it when they are hale and healthy. I love it when they are full of themselves and having a great and joyful life. I am cheering them on, always.

I realized this month that many people like it when the people around them are small.

That must be an awful feeling, to wish people ill, to want them to fail, to want them to be less than who they can be.

So this month, I had an opportunity to observe and contemplate the world of people. During this same time, I sat down and started to write my novel *Whackadoodle Times*.

I had a tough time at first. I had written the first chapter a few years earlier. I had really liked it, and I was afraid I couldn't keep going and have it be as good. In it, a homeless woman comes to live with a very rich family (at least that's what we think is going on); in exchange for room and board, the homeless woman promises to do one great thing a day.

Besides worrying about whether I could make the entire book good, I was stymied about the "one great thing a day" idea. I thought I needed to figure each "great thing" ahead of time, and I couldn't. That was my first concern.

My second concern was that the main character was not exactly admirable. She was a foul-mouthed adulterer. And she was rich. I didn't really want to be in her head space.

But she really wanted me to write her story. I balked, figured I'd write something else, but there she was. Ideas kept popping into my head like little word balloons from her saying, "See, wouldn't this be fun?"

She was funny, I'll give her that.

So I told myself I'd try it for 10,000 words.

I began writing.

All the emotional crap I'd been struggling with dropped away almost as soon as I began writing. And I wasn't aware of any of my physical stuff. If I felt crappy, I didn't notice while I wrote.

It turned out I didn't have to worry about the one "great thing." Each day (in the book) something happened that became the "one great thing." And I fell in love with the main character, Brooke McMurphy. I felt liberated as I wrote because she says pretty much anything and does pretty much anything. That was wonderful!

Of course, she was screwed up. She had so many problems, but I sympathized with her. She was surrounded by people who did not live up to her expectations, but mostly, she didn't live up to her own expectations.

I wrote this book more quickly than I'd ever written any other book. I never laughed as hard while writing a book as I did writing this one. In the end, I never cried so hard during the writing of a novel.

Each night I'd read a section to Mario, and he'd laugh. This gave me the confidence to keep going.

I finished writing it in about ten days, give or take. Then I went up to Sedona with my oldest and youngest sisters. We had such a good time. We didn't fight; we didn't have awkward silences. We talked and laughed and hiked and grossed each other out. It was fabulous.

When we came back to Scottsdale, I stayed overnight with my father and got to spend time with my dad, three of my sisters, and three of my brothers-in-law. It was a good visit. Once again, everyone seemed kind and funny and just nice to be around.

Back at the Sanctuary, I took a day off. But I had decided that I wanted to try and write another book. I had about ten days left before we were heading home. I could do it.

At first, I didn't know what I wanted to write. About twenty years ago, I wrote a mystery novel about the character Jane Deere. In that version, Jane had run away from her family when she was young, changed her name, and was living in a small town in Washington. Even though I loved her character (and the character of Dragon, her main squeeze), I didn't like the novel so I put it away. During this last summer, Jane had come knocking on my imagination again, only this time, she was living in Portland, Oregon.

Now while I was sitting in the Quail House figuring out what I'd write, Jane Deere came out of the woodwork: She was here in Tucson and her entire family thought she had died in a firebombed cottage twenty-years earlier.

So I began writing her story. When the events of the novel were going to take place in Portland, the novel was called *Doe*. But here in Tucson, the novel became *Pricked*. The title kept me thinking about the fairy tale, "Briar Rose," which happened to be one of my touchstone fairy tales. Years ago I had written a short story called "Briar Rose," and it was one of my most reprinted stories.

During the time I was working on *Pricked*, I read several versions of "Sleeping Beauty" and "Briar Rose." Even though my novel was not a retelling of "Briar Rose" or anything close to that, I felt like the essence of that tale was at the heart of this book.

I also came to believe that the essence of this tale was at the heart of my life.

For years, I have had this theory—unprovable thus far—that Western fairy tales may be coded instructions left by our ancestors. They were a way of preserving the Old Ways, but they were encoded so that the conquerors, the church, or the new dominant culture wouldn't know the truth of them; those who could figure out the key or code would. They were like pages of a Book of Shadows hidden in plain sight.

Even if this isn't true—and there's no research that indicates it is—I like thinking about it, and I like reading fairy tales with this in mind. (One day, perhaps, I'll do more with this idea.)

In any case, one night Mario and I went out to dinner and we read a version of "Briar Rose." He had never heard the Grimm's version before. We tried to look for hidden meaning in the tale. But we kept coming up with what seemed obvious: Don't disrespect the women, especially the old wise women. (Good advice.) Don't try to subvert fate because it's useless. (I'm all for trying to subvert fate or anything else.) Your prince will come. (I don't think so.)

I said let's look at the fairy tale the way some people look at dreams: Imagine that everything and everyone in it is the dreamer.

This made me contemplate the prince, which I hadn't done before because he seemed incidental. I hadn't cared about him. But now, I was thinking of him as the dreamer. The thorns were the dreamer. The spindle, Briar Rose, the king, queen, the prince: They were all the dreamer.

I realized that the prince didn't fight his way through the thorns. He happened to come along when the 100 year curse was over. He approached, the thorny hedge moved out of the way for him, and he stepped through. He walked into the palace where everything and everyone was asleep until he found Briar Rose's room. She was just waking up.

In the version Mario and I read, she was waking up when he entered the room. He didn't kiss her. He wasn't the hero. He just had great timing.

I kept thinking about this over the days that followed. I imagined that thorny hedge growing up to cover the palace and everyone inside. They were protected from the outside world during that 100 years. No one could hurt them, rob them, destroy anything.

But when the time was right, the thorny hedge moved aside and let the prince enter the palace grounds.

When the time was right, the princess woke up.

I walked the Sonoran Desert and looked at the thorny bushes and trees all around me. In most places, it looked impenetrable.

Often I have felt covered in the thorns of my suffering. Out here in the desert, surrounded by thorns, I became more aware of who I was and what my life had become. Was I inside my own thorny palace? Only I wasn't asleep, I was coming awake.

One day I wrote 7,000 plus words on *Pricked*. The next day I wrote 10,000 or thereabouts. It didn't feel like work. It felt like how it always feels when I'm in the flow: Like I was writing down what I saw and heard.

Each morning I did what I had done every day here. I'd step outside of the Quail House with my rattle, the one I had made last spring out of elk hide, a rosemary branch, and rabbit fur. I acknowledged the Mysteries, asked if they would co-create this day, this novel, and my good health with me. After my song, after my prayer to the elementals, I'd go inside and write.

I was feeling more and more free.

How can I explain? It felt physical. It felt soulful.

For a year or more I'd been trying this indie writing path.

I didn't worry about finding a publisher for my work. I didn't worry about the length of my books. I just let the stories come to me, and I wrote them down.

My true creativity was returning.

When I was a girl, I had written for the pure joy of it.

And I always wanted an audience. My mother introduced me to Emily Dickinson when I was a girl, and I loved her poetry. But I knew her story was not my story: I wanted my work to be read.

I used to say, "I'm not writing for my dresser drawers."

Now, in the Quail House, I felt as though I was writing for an audience, but it was not an audience of publishers, editors, or agents. I wasn't writing for the marketplace. I was writing for an audience of readers.

Writing *Whackadoodle Times* was one of the most joyful writing experiences I've ever had. And writing *Pricked* was equally as joyous for a different reason. It felt physically joyful. It's hard to explain. I was being transformed by these novels.

On the last day that I wrote on *Pricked,* I stood under the sun with my rattle in hand. I sang to the directions. I sang to the desert. I sang to the sun. As I did so, I saw in my mind's eye that thorny hedge covering the palace, that thorny hedge that staved off all intruders and visitors. Staved off all saviors, had there been one. I saw the thorny hedge move away, saw flowers blossom, saw the path leading into the palace. Into my heart? My healing? My own happiness.

Timing is everything.

I felt as though joy was bubbling up from the desert ground. I raised the rattle up high and sang. Now was my time. Now was the time for healing. Now was the time for success. My slumber was over; my suffering was over.

Timing is everything.

Time for healing.

I went into the Quail House and continued writing on *Pricked*. That evening, Mario came and sat with me as I wrote. I was completely in my imaginal world. For years I had thought it strange that I was the most comfortable in my stories. Wasn't that a sign of some kind of social deficiency?

No, no!

I have often said that I'm a stenographer to the imaginal worlds.

Now as I finished this book—my second completed novel in less than a month—I realized I wasn't just a stenographer: I was a mediator between this world and the imaginal worlds. I brought these stories out of there and into here.

The thorny hedge was moving. I looked out into the Sonoran Desert, the desert that had pricked me awake for the last eight winters, and I brought Jane Deere's story into the here and now.

When I wrote the last sentence, I stood up and cheered.

Wow. I had written a novel in five days.

Now it is our last night here at the Old Mermaids Sanctuary.

I first came here eight winters ago. This place has been a sanctuary for me. It has saved my life. I am a different person from the one who first came here. I was struggling inside my thorny palace, not comfortable with my thorns. Or anyone else's. Today many of the same issues haunt me that haunted me eight winters ago.

And yet, the stories are freer now.

I am freer now. I feel my true self rising again after a long painful slumber. It can't matter that anyone wants me to be small or wants me to be less than I can be. It can't matter. It's too high a price for companionship.

I'll tell the stories.

The rest will follow. Healing will follow.

That is my wish. My desire.

I wonder if I should redecorate the thorny palace or leave it all together?

I suppose if we imagine that Briar Rose was on a pilgrimage (albeit a sleepy pilgrimage) and now the pilgrimage is over, she must leave the palace.

And I must leave this thorny palace, this refuge.
So that I may be healed.
May I be healed, may I be healed, may it be so.
It is so.

Year Nine

The Monster's Daughter

THE MONSTER'S DAUGHTER: AN ESSAY

> I gift you with healing and magic.
> —*Sister Faye Mermaid*

> Perhaps all the dragons of our lives are princesses who are only waiting to see us once beautiful and brave. Perhaps everything terrible is in its deepest being something helpless that wants help from us.
> —*Rainer Maria Rilke*

December 19, 2012
I've been thinking about gifts today. And trials. Reality. And monsters.

What is real? What is true? What must we endure and what must we overthrow?

I don't believe in suffering for the sake of suffering. Of course we suffer. That is a given. But why cultivate it? And because someone suffers that does not mean they are holy, good, or divine. Suffering does not make us better. Lordy, no. Does suffering hone us? Make the sword that is us tougher, more magical, more efficient?

I don't know. I'm not a sword. I'm a human being.

If I suffer, if something bad happens to me, I am not a better human being. I'm just a human being who has suffered.

Maybe it depends upon what kind of person one is when something terrible happens. If it comes as a surprise, if it is totally and wholly unexpected suffering, perhaps we can't rise above it. Get over it.

I had a remarkably fortunate childhood. I was bonded to the land more than I was ever bonded to any human being. I watched for messages from the skies as I dug my bare toes into the damp earth. I fed the animals, wild and tame. I ran with the wild things.

My mother broke when I was quite young, and she never recovered. Neither did we. Is the soul of a family always the mother? As she goes, so goes the family?

I don't want to go there. Why? Because I find psychology tedious—watery—and not in a good way. I'm too old to be buffeted by childhood trauma.

And yet.

For years as child, I had merciless nightmares. They were so bad I would fight not to go to bed each night. When I slept, creatures came out of the woodwork and hunted me down. Or tried to. I was a runner—a marathoner—in my dreams. I could outrun any monster.

Except when I was the monster. In one dream I smiled while I spilled my guts. Literally.

As a girl, I tried to hold disparate realities in my mind, in my body, but it was difficult. Where did serial killers fit into my wilderness background? How did the outrageous acts of violence taking place in nearby Detroit, delineated on the nightly news, fit into my childhood? And the pristine river that ran behind our house—the river that flooded every winter and froze, becoming our winter water wonderland where I skated every chance I could get—why was it now unsafe to eat any fish or shellfish taken from it? Why did I see laundry bubbles on the surface of the water when I went down to the riverside?

I did my best. I saved other kids from bullies but became terrified one day when a teacher threatened to switch us all with a stick because she was pissed at us. I hid under the bed each morning for days, refusing to go to school because I said I was sick. Why didn't anyone believe me?

I wasn't sick: I was afraid. Of course, I never told my parents what was scaring me.

Perhaps fear is a form of sickness.

No, it's a protection, isn't it?

And when my animals began to die, I was awash with grief. My parents took me to a doctor and he gave me pills so I wouldn't be so upset.

Was that the message of the late sixties and early seventies? *Don't feel. But if you do, take a pill, baby.*

When I was a teen, I read books about the coming apocalypse via the atom bomb. I fantasized about making it to the mountains somewhere out west where I'd be safe from a nuclear holocaust.

We were all going to die from the pollution, a nuclear bomb, or some psycho hunting women. If we were afraid about any of it, please don't mention it; step to the side and take your pills, please, please.

And then I grew up. When I was still in my teens, just barely in college, a psychologist diagnosed me with post traumatic stress disorder. Only she didn't call it that because they didn't yet diagnose civilians with this particular disorder. She said I had all of the reflexes of a child who grew up in a war zone.

What?

She didn't really know how to help me, except more therapy.

How did talking about shit that happened when I was a kid help me feel better? So what if my mother was sick and my father was pissed and we were all just trying to do the best we could? *I had it fucking easy.*

How long after that did some medical doctor tell me I was allergic to the world?

Now THAT really did not help.

I refused to be allergic to the world.

This is my fucking world, buddy. I am not allergic to it.

And yet, I felt like crap.

I got married and Mario and I moved to the Oregon coast. While I was researching a novel, I learned more than I could quite fathom about pesticides and the dumping of toxic chemicals in developing countries. We were also part of a peace group, helping refugees from El Salvador. I couldn't come to grips with how seemingly cruel people were to one another. I was diagnosed again with post traumatic stress disorder. Years later, I wrote about this period of my life in a roman à clef, *Forks in the Road:*

> Yet the reality of what was happening to the environment and people was horrific. I wondered how anyone could know the things we now knew and not go crazy. I had always been overly empathetic. (Or just plain pathetic.) As a child, I cried when they cut down trees on the lot next door to us. I mourned the loss of those trees for years. When my dog was run over by a car I was depressed for months; my mom finally took me to a doctor, and he gave me what he called pep pills. My psyche could not take the onslaught of constant horror.
>
> Could anyone's?
>
> On the Oregon coast, I began to fall apart.
>
> One day I heard a bird cry out. A strange call. I went to the window and looked down at the side-

walk leading to our door. On the cement, half a snake twitched. It was so grotesque. Horrific in a way that only real life can be. I stood watching it for a while, wondering how it had gotten there, finally realizing a bird had most likely dropped half of the snake as it flew over. *The snake had lost its mind—and half its body.*

Soon after I lost my mind.

Me, middle-class white chick, began exhibiting classic symptoms of post-traumatic stress disorder.

I thought I was going insane. I could not read for a time; the letters kept moving on the page—and besides, the ideas were frightening. I had an anxiety attack that lasted a year. I hallucinated.

A doctor told me I was allergic to the world.

Whatever that meant.

The world was poison and my body was like a map of those poisons—or a container for poisons, he said.

No, no, I screamed silently. The world is more than poisons; I am more than poisons.

"You are like the canary in the mine," he said.

No. I refuse to be a fucking canary, singing the blues before dropping dead in my cage, feet sticking straight up to the sky.

I broke during that period of my life. Just like my mother had. Like her, I never recovered. And soon my life completely revolved around getting back to what I had been. Getting back to who I had been.

But that was an impossible task. We can never be what we were. Every single one of us has to endure something we wish we could avoid.

I am different than I would have been because of what has happened to me. Before, I was brilliant. I was beautiful. I thought I could do absolutely anything. I was going to save the world.

After, I wished the world would save me. I am no longer brilliant, at least not in the way I was. My mind isn't as quick as before. I was an amazing short story writer before. Now I can't seem to go to that deep place in a short piece of writing—it's too painful. I need to build up to it, which I can do when I write a novel. I would have never written *The Jigsaw Woman* before. Or *The Church of the Old Mermaids*. Certainly not *Ruby's Imagine*.

I knew more people before. I was better at relationships. Better in crowds.

Or maybe I wasn't. Who knows?

It doesn't actually matter.

Lately I've realized I have been focused on my wound. I thought because I tried to ignore it, because I didn't talk about it to family and friends, because I only wrote about it for people who were mostly strangers, because of all that, I figured I wasn't someone who was wallowing in my wounded-ness. I didn't blame my parents or my childhood. I felt angry and sad for moments of time, but then I would stuff those feelings as far down as I could.

I mean, really, what good would it do to feel anything?

Don't go deep, just stay in the shallows.

I've been wondering lately if perhaps as a culture we just don't go deep. We stay in the shallows. Because it is unseemly to feel things. And especially to feel things and then talk about them.

I'm not sure I feel much of anything these days except bad.

And that ain't good.

I hear this from many people.

Many beautiful things happen every day of my life. It seems

stingy not to feel joy at my fortune. But I think feelings just got in the way: How many years can one feel BAD. If we give away one feeling (the bad feeling), maybe the others go away, too?

Perhaps that is the greatest journey, the greatest task, to find again the treasure of our feelings.

Or at least *my* feelings.

When I was young, I believed I was put on this earth to love. I knew this was true because I was so good at it. Good at loving.

I'm not sure how good I am at it any more. Yet when I do feel that rush of love now, I feel completely WELL. Whole. Holy.

Some days I'm not sure how to put one foot in front of another. When I have no answers. When I can't let go and just be. I am so uncomfortable.

Perhaps I need to feel love for my suffering. Perhaps suffering is like some kind of monstrous parent trying to help us get through life.

Pick another way, strange parental unit.

I am tired of my wound. I don't want to pick at it any longer. I don't want to focus on it.

Perhaps I will go treasure hunting instead. Maybe learn to find treasure within.

And without.

Today I found some kind of aloe vera plant growing near the house here. I love aloe vera plants. I can't count how many times this plant has healed a part of my body. This particular plant, or bunch of plants, was blooming. I had never seen an aloe vera plant blooming and I was impressed. Coming up from the plump succulent leaves was a stalk and then apricot-colored trumpet-like blossoms fell away from the stalk. This plant was decidedly sexual. I grasped the closed blossoms in one hand and I could feel a kind of pulsing—throbbing? I smiled. Yep. I leaned over and felt the plump dark green leaves, carefully avoiding the tiny spikes on the edges.

I went and got Mario, and we stood together next to the plant. While we were gazing at the plant, we heard the unmistakable whir of a hummingbird, but when we looked toward it, it flew away and sat on a nearby cholla tree. She watched us, her head going back and forth, back and forth. I leaned against Mario, and without a word, we stepped back a bit, giving the hummingbird a clearer view of her intended: the aloe vera blossoms. Then we stayed very still. I closed my eyes and told her we intended no harm. We were peaceful, peaceful, peaceful.

Several minutes later, she flew toward us and the aloe vera blossoms. She dipped her beak up into this blossom and that blossom, her iridescent green feathers catching the sunlight on this cold morning. I stayed close to Mario, feeling his warmth and familiar heft. I listened to the hummingbird's wings—brrr, brrr, brrr. And I felt such joy and love. Love for this powerful little bird, for the sensual plant, for the earth beneath my feet and the blue, blue sky above, and for the man next to me.

Ahhh.

What a gift.

LANDED

February 2, 2013

It is our last day at the Old Mermaids Sanctuary. For the last nine winters, I have written a last essay, often on the last day. I attempt to put into words what this place and this time has meant to me. This is most likely our last visit here, although I've said that before. But this time it looks more and more like the place will be sold. This year I'm not certain what to say about this last visit.

Eight plus years ago, we found this place after I asked friends and acquaintances if they knew of an environmentally safe place in the Southwest where Mario and I could come for a few weeks a year. The Pacific Northwest winters were taking a toll on me, and I wanted some warmth and sunshine. Terri Windling answered my email, telling me she knew of a place that might just work. Nine winters ago, Mario and I arrived here and discovered a place of extraordinary beauty and mystery—and we fell immediately in love.

That first year, I planned on resting while Mario worked. I ended up writing 60,000 words of nonfiction. I sat under an old mesquite tree many evenings, telling stories to the tree and other Visibles and Invisibles as the sun went down. I am sitting under that same mesquite tree right now. It is ancient and beautiful and has roots that go all the way to China, or close to it.

The second winter we were here, the Old Mermaids came up out of the wash and told me their stories. Since then, we have called this place the Old Mermaids Sanctuary, or the Sanctuary. And that's what it has been for me these eight years. I look forward to coming here all year long. I believe I've written nine novels while I've been on the Sanctuary.

Away from the Sanctuary, these haven't been easy years. I struggled with illness and had two surgeries, both my careers faltered, my father had major heart surgery, a close relative battled drug addiction, one of my brothers-in-law had a severe stroke, Mario dealt with some health issues, my best friend died, two other close friends died suddenly and unexpectedly, and my mother died. One could argue that these are just the days of our lives, but because of my nearly constant anxiety, the normal travails of life often felt more unbearable than they needed to be.

As the years have gone by, life continued to get more difficult instead of easier for me, despite my nearly constant attempts to change, to fix what ails me. I have tried just about every healing modality known to humankind (and then some) and still, I wasn't improving. I studied shamanism and many different kinds of folk healing. Despite some improvements now and again, I was still sick and anxious. I started feeling resentful and morose. I used to think I was put here on this earth to love, but I didn't love much of anything or anyone any more, at least not with the joy and passion I had once had.

I didn't believe this was the life I was intended to live. (Intended by whom? Well, intended by me for one.) When I was younger, I wanted to help people, I wanted to change the world. Now, I just wanted to get well, be well. Whenever I would start seeing some kind of new practitioner, they were always optimistic and certain we could get to the heart of the problem to get me well. (Except Western medicine practitioners: They thought what was going on with me was chronic and I had to learn to live with it.) And then after a year or two into the process (whatever it was: therapy, naturopathy, etc.), the healer would say something like, "Perhaps this is just who you are." Or maybe I had a block or a miasm or some such.

I never accepted this. And I always thought if I was incurable, then I would accept it. Every person I know with a medical diagnosis for an illness they have has come to terms with their illness. Except me. I didn't believe it. Despite my own body's evidence to the contrary, I didn't believe I was chronically ill. Chronic means forever, right?

What mattered to me was good health. What mattered to me was a cure. When I'd read a book on healing or wellness, the authors would often say there was a difference between healing and being cured. And I'd think, "Bullshit. Obviously you have never been ill." I didn't want some pie in the sky healing where I thought everything was peachy-keen even though I was still sick.

Every time I returned to the Old Mermaids Sanctuary, I believed I would be healed. Every time I wrote a book, I believed I would be cured. And when I wasn't, I wasn't so much disappointed as I was perplexed. Because I believed with my whole body and soul that healing is much simpler than we realize. The best shamans, the best healers, the best doctors can heal with a nod, a gesture, a reminder: or by doing nothing at all.

Yes. So where was my nod?

When Mario and I first got to the Sanctuary this year, I had quite a few travails. The details don't matter, but I felt like I was being pummeled at every level of my being: physical, emotional, spiritual. After a week or more of wondering if we should just go home, I started reading book after book about healing modalities I hadn't heard of before. I tried every one of them. Sometimes the symptoms I was experiencing actually got worse. Sometimes they got marginally better.

I watched for signs. If a word or a phrase or a name caught my attention, I followed it through. I researched like crazy. I worked like crazy trying to find a formula to fix me.

I did a tarot reading with three cards. They turned out to be three major arcana cards. The World was me. The Tower was what was happening to me. The Star was how I could deal with the process. The Star is all about healing, completeness, hope, and intuition. In other words, I had done the work. Now let it beeee. I had been trying for so long, working so hard for so long: I needed to learn to let go. To do nothing.

Easier said than done.

I watched a video of Louise Hay called *You Can Heal Your Life*. Even though I hadn't found affirmations effective for me in the past, I've always felt affection for Louise Hay. She seems so loving (and she's an indie writer and publisher). She said after years of working with various affirmations and causes of illnesses with people, she discovered that when people learned to love and accept themselves, their lives turned around.

I had heard something like this before, of course, over the years. But I didn't believe it. I thought, I don't love and accept myself THIS way. Maybe if I was different THEN I could love and accept myself. But on this day as I watched the video, I realized I didn't not love other people because they were sick, so why wouldn't I love myself? I started talking to myself in the third person. "I'm so sorry you've had to go through this. That must have felt really bad. You've been very brave."

My spirits began to lift almost immediately.

I also started to think about who I am and what my life is. All of my life I have talked to the trees, rocks, the sky, plants, animals. I have also talked to that which is not there. But it's not something I advertised to other people. I wasn't embarrassed or ashamed of it, but I knew—especially when I was a child—that it wasn't something we talked about. (I was a child with a very vivid imagination, as I heard over and over.)

As an adult, I didn't talk about it because I never wanted to be considered flaky. I believed I was practical, tough, logical, and absolutely not one of those "airy fairy flakes." Yet I was one of those people who had "gut" feelings that often turned out to be accurate. I knew things that other people didn't seem to know. I did long distance healing on people—when I didn't believe in it—and people got better. And I often sensed things that I could never prove one way or another. For instance, I carried on long conversations with plants and with the spirits of the land or a place. I didn't know if these conversations were "real." Could I ever know?

As I struggled this time on the Sanctuary with so many physical problems, I decided to really try and let go and see what happened. (No, not try, just do.) Obviously I couldn't control everything, and the harder I tried the worse it seemed to get. So I closed my eyes and asked "what the hell is going on?" As I was asking this, an old plant friend of mine came and told me he wanted to show me something. I followed him down the wash to the fence the neighbors had put up across the dry riverbed a few years ago. He told me the fence was causing an energy blockage on the land. This time, instead of interrogating him on the truth or reality of what he was saying, I looked up and down the wash and I could "see" lines of light flowing up and down the wash in a kind of "x" pattern, only one "leg" of the pattern was slamming right into the metal pole of the fence.

I asked him what I could do. He told me to get some rocks and put them around the metal post in a kind of snaky line. I went around the wash asking rocks who wanted to be part of this venture and I picked up the ones who seemed to want to come. When I was finished, I ducked under the fence and continued walking in the wash. It felt completely different. For the first time since they'd put up the fence, the wash felt like a free flowing river. I closed my eyes and felt the Old Sea roll over me. It was glorious.

Within hours, many of my physical symptoms began to abate. Later in the day, Mario and I went to walk in the wash. We saw a rabbit on the way and I said, "It would be really nice to see your cousin the jackrabbit." We hadn't seen any jackrabbits this time. (We had never seen any on the Sanctuary.) Ten minutes later, two jackrabbits ran across the wash in front of us. On the way out of the wash, we said, "Wouldn't it be nice to see the owl before we leave?" We hadn't seen the owls here in a couple of years. A few hours later, an owl showed up on the Sanctuary, and we got to watch her for some time. (She showed up again the next day.)

Apparently on this day, wishes came true in the wash, so Mario and I returned and made other wishes.

Soon after I put the rocks around the fence, I returned to work on the novel I had started and stopped some days earlier *(The Monster's Daughter)*. I had gotten the idea for the novel just a few weeks earlier when we were driving down Highway 5 near Mount Shasta. Most of the novel takes place in California, near Mount Shasta.

Every year when we travel to Arizona, I make offerings to the land we pass through. I sing and say prayers. We stop at one lookout where I can whisper sweet somethings to Mount Shasta, and I usually leave a shell or a stone. Maybe this year the place decided they wanted the monster's daughter's story told and I was the one to tell it. I don't know, but I wrote 101,000 words and finished the novel in three weeks.

As the end of my time on the Sanctuary neared, I finally (again) decided that it doesn't matter if the world perceives me as flaky or airy fairy or whatever words they want to describe someone like me. Healing is in the invisible realms, right alongside magic, love, and joy—right beside the wild.

In Western culture, we want to name things. We want to codify and explain. We want rules for life. Do this and you'll succeed. Do that and you'll heal. But the mystery will not be codified or explained. I can't really explain where my novel came from or why placing stones in the wash coincided with the abatement of many of my symptoms. Does it matter?

I hear, feel, sense the call of the wild. That is what I do; that is who I am. Instead of running from that call, it is my life's work—my life's journey—to listen to that call and to sometimes interpret it. Sometimes I'll know what it means. Sometimes I won't. This means I must live on the edge of what is known and unknown, the edge of what can be explained and what is unexplainable. It also means I will live as part of the soul of the world. That is the only way I can fully survive, fully inhabit this body of mine.

I heard someone on the radio recently say that when we ask for healing, we need to be open to that which comes. We need to open our hearts. A few weeks ago, I bought a heart with a mirror at the center of it. Sometimes I look at it now and tell myself, "I love you." When I first started doing this, I'd see my face and wonder, "When did I get so old?" Now I just see myself grinning and think, "Years from now I'll thank myself for all the hard work I've been doing during these six weeks." Or maybe I'll thank myself for opening my heart and seeing the true beauty in myself.

I started writing this essay under the old mesquite tree. I had to leave and change my clothes because I had gotten thorns all over me. The first year I was here, I was constantly getting pricked by cactuses. This experience inspired my story "The Señorita and the Cactus Thorn." This year I keep thinking of Briar Rose. She was pricked awake. I feel like that this year. I've been pricked awake. Again. And again. Like, "Come on, Kim. GET IT. NOW."

I'm getting it. I'm getting it.

Life is more than stories. It is more than suffering. It is more. It is more.

One of the books I read this time said we needed to be more aware of our bodies to facilitate our healing. I said to Mario, "I am aware of every bit of suffering I feel. If I'm more aware of my body, it'll be worse."

He said, "More aware of the good things you feel in your body."

"Oh." Now that would be a new experience.

One day I was doing yoga and I suddenly felt the rug beneath my feet. I could feel the texture of it on my soles. It felt nice. I walked off the rug onto the cool stone floor. Mmmm. That felt nice, too. I padded around the casita for a few minutes, loving the feel of the stones and the rugs against my feet. It felt good.

It doesn't sound like much, but it was a beautiful moment for me.

I intend to string beautiful moment after beautiful moment together until there are more of them than non-beautiful moments. A string of beauty around my life.

I don't think I can sum up my nine winters here. Being here has changed my life. It has saved my life. And I am grateful for that.

And this year: What about this year? I feel transformed, transfigured, healed, and so much more. What I'm bound to heart and soul and body is still the wild land and everything that lives on it. (And this includes human beings, of course.) These bonds are not *binding* but liberating. The land makes us; we don't make the land. I am realizing that in my bones, finally. Maybe again.

This year I kept feeling the pull of the Catalinas. It felt like a kind of yearning, so I followed this yearning. We drove into the mountains and stopped at a high plateau overlooking the desert floor. As we stepped out onto the blond rock, a tiny snake slithered past us. A snake at 7,000 plus feet in the middle of the winter. We took this as an auspicious sign.

Through the binoculars, we could see the Sanctuary far below us. Gorgeous manzanita trees twisted up from the rocks. I bowed down to them. Stunted evergreen trees likewise rose up from the rocks. They were older than the hills—or close to it. Amidst the beauty was garbage. Normally this reality would have thrown me into melancholy. Instead I whispered an apology and left a song as a gift. (And next time, I'll bring gloves and a garbage bag.)

At one point, two young men ran all around us, oblivious to the church-like silence most people were maintaining. They huffed and puffed and scrambled onto and off of this rock and that rock, speaking in a language I didn't recognize. Every time they leaped dangerously from rock to rock, I prayed for their safety. And I smiled at their exuberance. For them, this sacred place must have inspired their bodies to run, jump, and huff and puff. Yes. What a place requires or wants can be different depending upon the person.

Of course.

Instead of being angry or annoyed with them I loved these loud boys. Ahhh. Finally. My heart was opening again.

What does this all mean?

Perhaps I am finally awakening to the truth of my life. To the truth of the world?

At the end of *The Monster's Daughter,* my main character Emily says, "But Papa, I am so awake."

Perhaps that sums it up for me, too. That is how I leave this place this year: I am awakening. It's as if I've been on a long space voyage. I slept and dreamed through the entire thing. Now I've landed. And I am awake.

Perhaps I am now awake and full of my true self.

And who am I?

I am the Witch who lives at the edge of the village. I am the Crazy Woman who hugs trees and talks to crows. I am the Old Woman who bargains with Weather Spirits and dances with the East Wind. I am the Crazy One who dreams a healing for you or for him. I am She Who Talks With That Which Is Not There. I am the One Who Sings Worlds Into Being.

I am the stenographer to the imaginal realms.

That is who I am.

ABOUT THE AUTHOR

Kim Antieau has written many novels, short stories, poems, and essays. Her work has appeared in numerous publications, both in print and online, including *The Magazine of Fantasy and Science Fiction, Asimov's SF, The Clinton Street Quarterly, The Journal of Mythic Arts, EarthFirst!, Alternet, Sage Woman,* and *Alfred Hitchcock's Mystery Magazine*. She was the founder, editor, and publisher of *Daughters of Nyx: A Magazine of Goddess Stories, Mythmaking, and Fairy Tales*. Her work has twice been shortlisted for the James Tiptree Award and has appeared in many best-of-the-year anthologies. Critics have admired her "literary fearlessness" and her vivid language and imagination. Her first novel *The Jigsaw Woman* is a modern classic of feminist literature. She is also the author of a science fiction novel, *The Gaia Websters* and a contemporary tale set in the desert Southwest, *Church of the Old Mermaids*. *Broken Moon*, a novel for young adults, was a selection of the Junior Library Guild. She has also written other YA novels, including *Deathmark, Mercy, Unbound, Ruby's Imagine,* and *The Blue Tail*. Kim lives in the Pacific Northwest with her husband, writer Mario Milosevic. Learn more about Kim and her writing at www.kimantieau.com.